American Quiltmaking

American Quilter's Society
P. O. Box 3290 • Paducah, KY 42002-3290
www.AQSquilt.com

To the quilters who have nourished our rich history,
given life to our art,
and graciously paved the way for our shared future in quilting.

AMERICAN
Quiltmaking
1970 – 2000

ELEANOR
LEVIE

Located in Paducah, Kentucky, the American Quilter's Society (AQS) is dedicated to promoting the accomplishments of today's quilters. Through its publications and events, AQS strives to honor today's quiltmakers and their work and to inspire future creativity and innovation in quiltmaking.

EDITOR: PATRICIA STATEN
GRAPHIC DESIGN: AMY CHASE
COVER DESIGN: MICHAEL BUCKINGHAM
QUILT PHOTOGRAPHY: CHARLES R. LYNCH AND RICHARD WALKER (unless otherwise noted)
STILL-LIFE PHOTOS OF FABRICS, TOOLS, AND PROCESSES: JOHN P. HAMEL

Library of Congress Cataloging-in-Publication Data

Levie, Eleanor.
    American quiltmaking : 1970-2000 / by Eleanor Levie.
        p. cm.
    Includes bibliographical references.
    ISBN 1-57432-843-3
    1. Patchwork. 2. Quilting. 3. Quilts. I. Title

    TT835.L465 2004
    746.46'0973--dc22

                            2004005406

Additional copies of this book may be ordered from the American Quilter's Society, PO Box 3290, Paducah, KY 42002-3290, or online at www.AQSquilt.com.

Contents

Foreword

How quiltmaking caught the fancy of liberated women in the 1970s is the story of *American Quiltmaking: 1970-2000* by Eleanor Levie. Now thirty-some years old, this so-called "quilt revival" feels more like a quilting boom with no end in sight. For many of us, myself included, this book is an insider's view of the workings of our quilt revival. For others, it's an invitation to get on board!

Eleanor Levie's personal history parallels this end-of-century quilt phenomenon. She learned to sew (but not quilt) from her mother in 1960, and decorated her hippie-era clothes with patchwork in 1970. In 1978, she embarked on an editing career in New York City. Through her work, she witnessed firsthand the rise of quilting at the end of the twentieth century. She collaborated with the leading quilt designers, writers, and manufacturers, many of whom she has reached out to for their perspectives on the development of the quilt industry.

A retrospective such as this would have made my research of the 1920s and '30s quilt revival a lot more interesting. For example, I was always curious about the decision makers—the fabric manufacturers, contest organizers, pattern designers, and sales managers. My best source of contemporary accounts was newspapers and magazines, but scrolling through microfilm gets old quickly. If I was lucky, I came upon a box of fabric blocks, patterns, kits, or even some correspondence.

I remember a February, 1928, *Modern Priscilla Magazine* with an article on the needlework page with this intriguing title, "A Placid Old Art Invades Our Hurrying Age." In 1928, *Modern Priscilla* was competing for the same readers as *Ladies Home Journal's*—middle-class, well-educated urban women. The article by Gertrude Shockey explained how "Modern manufacturers are co-operating with modern quilters even to reproducing the old time calico prints as staunch and strong in color as the originals. There are books and magazines galore offering instruction and inspiration for quilting and quilts—for this placid art has somehow captured the fancy of this hurrying age." The scene Gertrude Shockey described sounded similar to today's quilt world. She also seemed a little surprised at the sudden popularity of quiltmaking in the Roaring Twenties—wondering how it "somehow captured" an audience.

Quilter's Newletter Magazine and International Quilt Market & Festival, sponsors of the 2000 Quiltmaking in America survey, reached similar conclusions—surprising to some, but not to them. "Quilting, a craft born of necessity, is now a bona fide art form beloved by nearly 20 million adult Americans who spend a staggering $1.84 billion per year on their hobby."

To those outside the quilt world, these are staggering numbers prompting a follow-up question, "How did a homely craft become a two-billion-dollar industry?" That is the core question Eleanor Levie attempts to answer. She points out the technological advances, large and small, in textiles, notions, sewing machines, and even computers. She explains how a simple rotary cutter and a cutting mat freed quilters from endless, tedious projects, and, by the way, it resulted in sales of a lot more fabric—106.6 million yards in 1991, according to the 2000 survey, enough to circle the globe 2.5 times!

A 1934 catalog entitled *Romance of the Quiltmaking Sales*, published by Stearns & Foster Co., the makers of Mountain Mist® batting, explained how the sale of one roll of batting resulted in $5 to $10 in extra sales of fabric and notions. They encouraged in-store quilt displays and quilt contests to heighten interest in quiltmaking. Obviously, marketing and technology have played a role in both revivals.

Both revivals also created "quilt celebrities" such as Eleanor Burns, whose quilt career is not so different from Ruby McKim, who designed patterns and cleverly marketed patterns via media outlets in the 1920s and '30s. McKim wrote for *Better Homes & Gardens* and the daily newspapers. Burns has her own television program and lectures widely. Both sold their patterns and products themselves.

The Dear Jane® quilt phenomenon born in the mid-1990s is not so far removed from Florence LaGanke's Nancy Page Quilt Club running in daily newspapers in the late 1920s and '30s. Nancy Page, a pen name for Florence LaGanke, convened a weekly club in the newspaper where members discussed a particular pattern and what colors and fabrics to use. Newspapers sponsored exhibitions of the finished Nancy Page quilts made in their towns. Today, Dear Jane quilt enthusiasts keep in touch via the Internet to discuss progress on their quilts and also enter quilt competitions at local and national levels.

Contests have played a major role in the current revival. Eleanor Levie calls the awarding of the $10,000 prize to a machine-made quilt (CORONA II: SOLAR ECLIPSE by Caryl Bryer Fallert) at the 1989 AQS Show a "watershed moment," for she believes it allowed quilters to experiment, make things quickly, and, most importantly, finish projects.

I am reminded of the judges' decision at the 1933 National Quilt Contest sponsored by Sears Roebuck & Co. Although the company offered a bonus to a quilt made in the theme of the Chicago World's Fair, no final round judges deemed those quilts worthy of the top prize. If they had, they might have signaled to quiltmakers of the 1930s that innovation in quilt design was encouraged. Art quilts as we know them might have emerged before the 1980s.

Instead, enthusiasm for making quilts stalled due partly to the paper and fabric shortages of the Second World War, but even in the post-war era, women's magazines steered clear of quilting features. With little attention given to quilts and their heritage, a break resulted in the tradition of mother teaching daughter to make quilts. Instead, home sewing of children's clothes, curtains, and slipcovers was encouraged. Ironically, the children born of that era—the same generation that lived through the Vietnam War, civil rights campaigns, and the women's libera-

tion movement—discovered quilts in the 1970s and returned them to center stage. This new generation, emboldened with hard-won personal freedoms, embraced quiltmaking as easily as others climbed the corporate ladder. In quiltmaking, they found opportunities to express themselves in cloth. They found like-minded, supportive women. Some even changed careers in midstream, opening quilt shops, and embarking on lucrative careers of writing and designing.

Today, a new wave of quilters is extending and enriching America's quiltmaking tradition—in a sense, they are the next invasion of our "hurrying age." Could their experience be any more exhilarating than the thirty years chronicled by Eleanor Levie? I suspect the answer is yes.

Merikay Waldvogel
Knoxville, Tennessee

Acknowledgments

This book, a celebration of the support and creativity of American quiltmakers in recent history, would not have been possible without the support of many creative individuals. First and fervently, I would like to express my loving thanks to my hubby, Carl Harrington. My best supporter—and my best critic—Carl helped me organize every chapter, and carried me through this chapter of my career, emotionally as well as financially. I must also recognize the contributions of our son, Sam. Worrying about this young robot-builder wielding power tools in the basement certainly took my mind off the pressures of writing this book!

I owe a debt of gratitude to many professionals in the quilt world for their friendship and help. Judy Roche, who could have written this book (and probably should have), opened treasure troves of recollections, fabrics, quilting supplies and books to me. The perspectives and perceptions of this quilter, collector, historian, and fabric designer were absolutely invaluable. In addition, I am grateful to quilter-extraordinaire Corienne L. Kramer, antiques dealer James W. Carroll, quilt-guild sister Nancy Lacey, author and editor Deborah Harding, Silver Stars Jean Ray Laury and Marti Michell. All generously loaned me "period" fabrics, swatches, quilts, magazines, books, and other oldies-but-goodies.

My respect and appreciation go out to many editorial talents. Mary Seehafer Sears polished my prose and propped up my ego. Her brilliant copywriting skills made me oh so glad I decided to "Farm It Out" (Mary's freelance business name). Of course, I would never have started in on a quilt history were it not for the invitation of the American Quilter's Society. I thank Publisher Meredith Schroeder, for her vision and faith in me, and Executive Editor Barbara Smith for shepherding me through the AQS process with patience and grace. Associate Publisher Jay Staten was instrumental in moving this project forward, and Editor Pat Staten patrolled my text for clarity and an ever-inclusive tone. I am honored to have had inestimable feedback on my manuscript from Bonnie Browning and Helen Squire at AQS, and from two other dignitaries of the quilt world: Gerald E. Roy and Merikay Waldvogel.

Furthermore, I am indebted to those artisans who lent their creative expertise to making this book a special delight to look through. My photographer, John P. Hamel, lavished care and imagination on everything I set up, despite the enormous number of shots and the small amount of time. Kudos to AQS photographers Charles R. Lynch and Richard Walker, and to Amy Chase for the interior design and layout.

I hereby acknowledge that time, space, resources, and my own fallibilities are all certain to keep this book from being a comprehensive account of the period between 1970 and 2000. Of course, no one book could do justice to every person, event, and quilt deserving of our attention. Apologies aside, I pay tribute to everyone who warmly responded to my calls for information and images. To all these wonderful resources—whether or not they are mentioned or quoted, and whether or not their work appears in this book—I thank them for sharing their memories and masterpieces with me.

Introduction

This is an abridged guide to the world of quilts and quilters during the last three decades of the twentieth century. I promise you won't find this book to be some dry old history textbook, because it's filled with loving memories and plenty of giggles. For those of us who have been quilting for a while, it is a fond trip down memory lane. Hopefully, you'll take a path you haven't traveled before and explore a different part of the quilt community. For you new sightseers, let me take you by the hand and show you the territory. In any case, you don't have to keep to a strict itinerary! There's no need to read from start to finish—simply meander wherever you like; proceed at your own pace. Everywhere along the tour, you'll discover how and why quilting has become so amazing, you'll find a lot of personal stories from some of the most respected and best-loved talents in the business, and you'll see quilts that will blow you away.

The friendliness of the quilting community is the key theme of this book. Certainly, my research was wide in scope. I poured over just about every issue of *American Quilter* and *Quilter's Newsletter Magazine* and stacks of books that came out between 1970 and 2000, which included the best selling how-to's and the beautiful quilt collections. But the real joy of this book is the patchwork of recollections distilled from dozens of interviews with the contemporary pioneers and leaders in the quilt world. Like almost everyone in the quilting community, they live up to their reputation for being the nicest people in the world. I know you'll enjoy reading their stories and getting their points of view, which will also enrich your understanding of the amazing things that happened in the quilt world between 1970 and 2000. I know you'll understand if on some rare occasion someone's memory of the 1970s, '80s, or even '90s is a tiny bit faulty. Just keep a few grains of salt handy, and be very glad they are sharing their memories as well as their wonderful quilts with us.

As you read this, I'm probably looking ahead to my next quilt, as perhaps you are, too. In pursuing this pleasure, we're linked to the past, savoring the same things that gave quiltmakers immense satisfaction in every era of history. Who could ask for anything more?

The Quilting Community: Camaraderie & Communication

THE QUILTERS (77" × 62", 1994)
by Marlene Brown Woodfield.
Photo by the artist.

"Who would like to help me make a quilt?" Irene Preston Miller asked in a casual way, back in 1970. Friends in Croton-on-Hudson, New York, all said "Oh, yes!" right away. An expert quilter, Irene had designed a pictorial album quilt in 1969, with the goal of raising both money and awareness to keep the Hudson River clean and scenic. Right from the beginning, this was to be a top-quality project, made exclusively from 100 percent cotton fabrics and completely hand-stitched. Irene scoured the Lower East Side in New York City, where she made buying trips for her fabric and yarn shop, until she found a few precious bolts of cotton in solid blues and greens. She gave every willing participant some of each fabric, which would tie all the blocks together, along with appliqué lessons for anybody who asked. Next, Irene assembled the blocks with sashing and borders and placed the quilt top onto an old Pennsylvania quilt frame in her shop. "It was a tight squeeze," Irene recalls. "Often, people had to climb under the frame to get to the other side in order to quilt a particular square." But all the time and effort spent on the HUDSON RIVER QUILT were certainly worth it. The completed piece received a flood of admiration, and in 1972 it fetched an unprecedented $23,100 at an auction to benefit the Hudson River cleanup.

To Bee, or Not to Bee

"Gatherings" have always been as important to quilters as quilts themselves. For three centuries in America, quilting was pursued within a family or a tight-knit community, or both. One generation passed its skills to the next.

Women worked together to mount their individual creations onto a frame, then sat around the frame to hand-quilt together. At these quilting bees, they shared their templates, the secrets to their needle skills, and the patterns and quilting traditions that had been in their families for generations. This was an opportunity for the generations to communicate on all topics, and to teach the value of helping others.

There was never a time in American history when women did not make quilts, alone or in small groups. During the colonial period, women needed to gather together for company and support just as much as they needed the quilts to help their families survive difficult winters. Collective nostalgia for this time fueled three major revivals, when the passion for quilting peaked. The first was 1860–1880, when the country

HUDSON RIVER QUILT
(95¼" x 80", 1972). In the collection of the
American Folk Art Museum, NYC,
a gift of the J. M. Kaplan Fund.
Photo by Matt Hoebermann.

was literally piecing itself back together after the Civil War. The second was during the 1930s, the Depression era, and again when people badly needed to recall the good old days. Newspapers, such as the *Kansas City Star*, offered weekly block patterns, and fabric manufacturers were producing cotton fabrics in fresh, new colors and whimsical prints, all welcome fodder for sharing amid economic hardships. The third revival began in the 1970s ... and is still going strong.

So what happened between the '30s and the '70s? In the 1940s, many women were working those jobs left by men marching off to war. Sewing was for the troops, and there were too many fabric shortages for anything else. During the '50s and '60s, most women shifted their priorities to post-war domesticity in suburbia, but quilting was still on the wane. Days were centered on the house and the kids. Women who liked to sew made curtains, A-line skirts, and kids' costumes, and evenings found women joining their families in front of the TV, rarely involved in quiltmaking. Husbands in middle management got transferred, families were scattered, and access to the older generation was limited. A generation of quilters was skipped, and the continuity of quilters from one generation to the next nearly disappeared.

America's Big Birthday

But then, as the 1970s began and the bicentennial approached, countless people took an interest in their roots and in exploring connections with the generations who came before them. Almost every quilt historian, and certainly every one who started quilting in the early to mid-1970s, can attest to the influence America's 200th birthday had on quilting. As a celebration of our history, this event grounded everyone in the values of roots and traditions.

In the early 1970s, in countless towns across America, quilts became banners to herald and celebrate the bicentennial. Historical societies and bicentennial committees asked quilters to help reawaken nostalgia with this most visual and tactile medium. Quilts helped reconnect Americans to their past with a declaration of individual and national pride.

Women with needle skills and time volunteered to work on group quilts, stitching patriotic spirit in cloth to herald local commemorations. This was especially true in Boston, and other birthplaces of the Revolution. "For the quilt world, the importance of the bicentennial cannot be overemphasized," says Richard Cleveland, founder of the Vermont Quilt Festival.

Lacking a mother, aunt, or even a neighbor or friend to show them the way, many women began to figure out quiltmaking on their own. Increasing experience and skills led to pride as surely as it had for previous generations. Yet, no matter how self-satisfying quilting could be, there was always a yearning for recognition of one's abilities and accomplishments.

Corienne Kramer was lucky enough to have quilters in her family who have complimented her workmanship since she began quilting as a teenager in the

The Bicentennial Star quilt pattern from Mountain Mist®, plus swatches of commemorative fabrics.

late 1960s, but she craved more of a response. She got it many years later when she fell into a group of quilters and quilt lovers who got together casually at each other's homes in Bucks County, Pennsylvania. "Someone would always be sharing an image of a quilt they saw in a museum, showing a new technique she had discovered, and showing her latest quilt project," Corienne says. "In contrast to the brief 'oh wow' accolades I had been getting, I now heard much more thoughtful responses, like 'That border is an interesting touch' and 'What made you put that blue there? It would never have occurred to me to do that.' I could always tell that these women were really taking notice and appreciating what I'd done."

The hunger for connection and validation spurred on a quilting revival like never before. Soon, women were joining quilting groups and guilds in droves, scouting out classes and workshops, and chartering buses to attend big quilt shows. They purchased the latest how-to books and subscribed to quilting magazines. As TVs and computers proliferated in homes, media connections were inevitable with quilt shows on TV and sharing ideas on the Internet. The quilting community rose up, stronger and larger than ever before. A Quilting in America 2000™ survey, commissioned by Primedia and Quilts, Inc., reported close to twenty million quilters over the age of 18, an industry with an annual worth of $1.84 billion. Indeed, the explosive growth of quiltmaking during the last three decades of the twentieth century was different from any previous revivals. Even during times of economic uncertainty, this latest revival was nothing short of phenomenal.

Bonding & Building

In 1970, seven women in the Washington, D.C., area founded The National Quilting Association, Inc. (NQA), a nonprofit organization run "by quilters for quilters ... to create, stimulate, maintain, and record an interest in all matters pertaining to the making, collecting, and preserving of quilts." The first NQA quilt show was held in the Greenbelt (Maryland) Public Library in September 1970, where there was not even room to hang quilts to their full length. Eventually, shows were held in an entirely different location around the country every year, making this the longest running annual quilt show in America. From small beginnings, the NQA grew, adding local chapters, a quilt registry, certification programs for teachers and judges (in 1979), recognition for masters of quilting, and education and scholarship programs.

But back in the early 1970s, while the NQA was young and before other quilting organizations existed, most quilters simply sought each other out, wanting to share their family quilts and those in their local historical societies. Just as happened a century ago, quilters gathered in homes or the meeting rooms of historical societies or churches. Frequently, the common goal was to make a commemorative bicentennial quilt for display in their town. Months later, when the quilt was completed and the accolades were but a memory, the groups continued. They were delighted to share their skills and inspiration

"This time, the resurgence shows no sign of waning. I firmly believe that quiltmaking has been permanently installed as an intrinsic part of American culture."

-Cuesta Benberry

"Of course, it's wonderful when Mother thinks your work is beautiful and your sister-in-law (who has never quilted) thinks your work is very nice (though admittedly your colors are a tiny bit weird). But real confirmation comes from the person who has a true dedication to the craft. Another quilter who shares your passion can offer the confirmation you need, and that means an attentive ear, an ear that really hears what you're saying because of similar experiences."

-Jean Ray Laury
from Quilter's Newletter Magazine

"There's nothing quite as rewarding as standing before your local quilt guild to show your newest finished or unfinished quilt. It spurs one on to make the next quilt even better than the last."

-Irma Gail Hatcher

with others. And women with time and interest joined the ranks, eager to learn the skills they hadn't received at the knees of their mothers or grandmothers.

These quilters formed support groups. In some groups, women could quietly sit and stitch together on individual projects or around a quilting frame. For women looking to assert their creativity, it was a chance to share information and constructive criticism, and to grow as artists. No matter how traditional or feminist the bent of the group, it provided an environment for venting worries about family members and personal problems, for finding acceptance, approval, and advice. These rewards were often the most highly prized thing to come out of these quilting get-togethers. In a Sit-'n-Stitch, women felt validated and supported.

The late 1970s and early 1980s saw the rise of the quilt guilds. Encouragement in these guilds always went well beyond quilting. Members sent out get-well cards, printed recipes for the popular treats served at refreshment breaks and annual pot-luck dinners, set up gift exchanges on a regular basis between "secret sisters" and annually at Christmas time. Such ongoing support was a key draw for those women who faced frequent relocations. A quilter and army officer's wife, Barbara Eikmeier was uprooted frequently throughout the 1980s and 1990s. "I always looked to a quilting group to ease the social difficulties of these military moves," she says. Whether her husband was stationed in Hawaii, Kansas, or Korea, she would immediately join the local guild. With every relocation, Barbara drew on the regional influences, while keeping up her old friendships through the mail and e-mails.

Barbara Eikmeier happens to be a talented and accomplished quilter, but neither quilting ability nor experience was ever required in the growing numbers of quilting groups. Novices were warmly welcomed into the fold, and the prevailing democratic attitude was that everyone was learning together. Since quiltmaking carries with it a wide range of skills, there has always been something for everyone's skill level and taste, from beginner to advanced. Anyone, at anytime, could start at the beginning, and there was usually someone with the proficiency to teach whatever the novice wanted to learn. Especially good teachers became recognized for their skills, and often traveled to other guilds, wrote books, or appeared on TV.

Guild It and They Will Come

By the mid-1980s, the majority of quilters probably enjoyed membership in guilds or groups. In 1986, *American Quilter* magazine ran a survey, and 69 percent of the respondents indicated affiliations to regular quilt gatherings. Some quilters met weekly, others monthly, enjoying the special pleasures of learning and quilting together. With more people involved, there were more ways to inspire each other. "Show 'n Tells," where members lined up to display their latest accomplishments, became the most popular feature of guild meetings.

Show 'n Tells exploded into annual or biennial guild-sponsored quilt shows, bringing recognition and prestige for the guild and for quilting in general. Sometimes quilting eclipsed other needle-art forms. Take, for example, the Cabin Fever Quilters' Guild, which organized in Fairbanks, Alaska, in 1979. In their very first summer, they convinced county fair organizers to include a quilt exhibition. That display was so well received by the public that, the next year, the quilts were taken out of the needlework division and given their own category.

Guilds also held economic power. Members paid dues, raffled off group quilts, and put on their own shows, where they charged admission and sold quilted projects, craft items, and baked goods. These shows, with exhibits of antique and new quilts, also brought publicity, which helped grow the membership. Sometimes a guild would raise money for charities; other times they used their collective funds to bring in professional teachers for regular programs of education and inspiration. Neighboring guilds coordinated the scheduling of an instructor, so they could share the cost of reimbursing her for transportation. On occasion, a guild would get a grant from their state arts council, allowing them to pursue bigger projects.

Of course, guilds used quilts as payment for use of a meeting place or exhibition site. Many towns, historical societies, hospitals, nursing homes, churches, and libraries were the lucky recipients of a commemorative quilt in payment for use of a site. Local, regional, and even major quilt shows were founded, supported, and staffed by active guild volunteers.

HAWAII ROUND ROBIN (52" x 52", 1991) by round-robin participants with Barbara J. Eikmeier, coordinator.
Photo by the artist.

But the guilds never seemed to lose their own identity and inclusiveness. In addition to the supportive Show 'n Tells came the stimulating guild challenges—projects with a special twist that encouraged participants to stretch and grow, by using, for instance, a specific color palette, type of fabric, or theme. In the late 1980s, some quilting groups within guilds initiated the

Round Robin, sometimes called the Merry-Go-Round. One person in the group would make a center medallion or other focal portion of a quilt top, and others would add successive borders around it. The result was usually a delightful surprise to the quilter who started things off. Then, at the end of the 1990s, many guilds were intrigued by a regular mystery quilt project. A series of how-to's for assembling pieces of blocks were handed out at various guild meetings, setting up a competition to see who could figure out the emerging pattern first.

Group quilts were also de rigueur with guilds. If one member excelled at design, she might mastermind a large project, usually involving members doing repeat blocks in a given color scheme. The Tuesday Night Friends quilting group of Ann Arbor, Michigan, which has been in existence since 1980, was inspired to try a different way of putting together a group quilt. The project was conceived when several members of the group admired a group quilt at the 1997 American Quilter's Society (AQS) Quilt

IN THE GARDEN (86½" × 81", 1998) by the Tuesday Night Friends with Sue Holdaway-Heys as facilitator and coordinator. Photo by Sue Holdaway-Heys.

Show and Contest in Paducah, Kentucky, and one of them, talented quilt artist Sue Holdaway-Heys, noticed that the quilt had been constructed in sections. Sue suggested they try such a project. After another member found the perfect picture for inspiration, Sue became the coordinator. Members worked in pairs on nine different blocks, or panels, which Sue assembled like a giant Nine-Patch. Other members added additional appliqué and embroidery, and helped baste the top and machine-quilt it. IN THE GARDEN was the idyllic landscape that resulted, and it won awards at five different national shows.

Diving In, Via Mainstream Magazines

For people who did not have a quilting group, let alone a mother, grandmother, or a friend to inspire and teach them, magazines and books brought many new converts to quilting. In the 1970s and early 1980s, popular women's magazines were showcasing quilting projects. Their editors had been wowed in

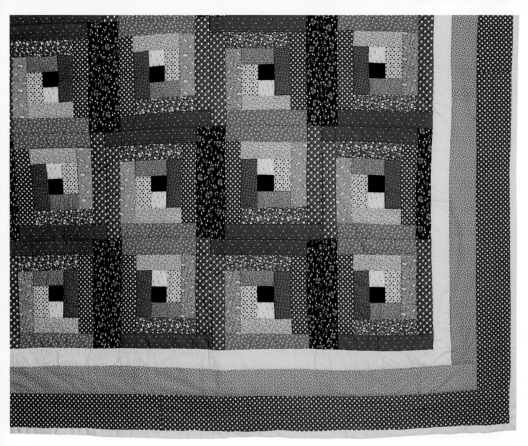

QUICKEST QUILT IN THE WORLD (detail)
(1976) by Marti Michell.
Photo by John P. Hamel.

the summer of 1971, when the Whitney Museum of American Art in New York City exhibited pieced quilts collected by Jonathan Holstein and Gail van der Hoof (see Historic Connections, page 112). *House Beautiful* declared patchwork "the darling of the day." *House & Garden* also featured quilts and home decorating accessories printed with quilt motifs.

Magazines made patchwork hot. Catering to the masses of middle-American women on a budget, *Ladies' Home Journal, Good Housekeeping,* and *Redbook* all included how-tos for quilts and other crafts. The public loved the look. The only trouble was that most people were hard pressed to devote a lot of time to quiltmaking, especially when it involved installing a big frame and quilting on one.

In 1977, Marti Michell brought a promotional idea to Gloria Golden at *Woman's Day* magazine. She suggested that the magazine offer its readers a Log Cabin quilt kit done in a stitch-and-flip technique that eliminated the need for a quilting frame. Gloria recognized the potential of this idea right away and had Marti make a quilt that weekend. *Woman's Day* called it the "quickest quilt in the world." As Marti recalls, "It was an unbelievable success, a blockbuster. The magazine ran an ad featuring this type of quilt five different times, each time in a different color palette. My husband Dick and I handled the fulfillment, and we had UPS trucks—18-wheelers—pull up to deliver fabrics and take away kits. I don't know how many trucks we filled, or how many millions of dollars worth of kits were sold, but it was incredible." With one simple quilt design, countless women went from wanting the patchwork look to getting it.

"The timing was perfect. Quilts had never before grown into national consciousness in such fertile soil, or seemed to symbolize so many different things to people of such opposing viewpoints."

-Penny McMorris
From The Art Quilt

At the same time, *Family Circle* magazine, with a readership of over six million, found that magazine covers with quilts got high approval ratings from readers. Deborah Harding, who was the needlework and crafts editor at *Family Circle*, says, "It was always a toss-up between featuring a chocolate cake or a quilt on the cover. Both had an amazing ability to boost magazine sales."

All this exposure in popular women's magazines certainly heightened the visibility of quilting. Jean Ray Laury, who designed quilts for several magazines, generalizes about the work that appeared at that time: "Having quilts in magazines in the '60s and '70s was great ... I think it put the idea of making contemporary quilts right into the home. It made them accessible to everyone. It helped many women get started." Adds Deborah Harding, who frequently assigned editorial projects to Jean, "I also think this kind of mainstream coverage—reaching millions of households—was also a corporate wake-up call to fabric, thread, batting, and sewing-machine manufacturers. At

February and October 1974 issues of *Family Circle*. Quilts by Jean Ray Laury. Photos for *Family Circle* by Rudy Muller.

that time, the focus was on pattern companies that specialized in dress patterns. These were the heydays of *Simplicity*, *Butterick*, and *McCall's*. Quilting, or anything to do with home decorating, was considered a stepchild at best, that is, until they realized how popular quilting had become."

By the mid-1980s, the quilt world was growing like a snowball rolling downhill. But dedicated quilters felt that some mainstream magazine projects played up the quick and easy theme too much. Jean Ray Laury reminisces, "Time got so important ... everything had to be done in fifteen minutes. That's the way article headlines were often written: 'Make a quilt in eight hours!' It missed an important part of quiltmaking—the contemplative, centering time provided by handwork." So quilters started to look to other media forms.

Magazines Just for Quilters

Those quilters eager for patterns and information could turn to *Quilter's Newsletter Magazine*, begun in 1969 on a shoestring. Bonnie Leman had been running a mail-order business for quilters out of her home, which enabled her to supplement the family income while raising her large family. She started a newsletter merely as a special service to her customers. For each of the first few issues, Bonnie explained, she re-rolled each page in the typewriter to type over and darken each letter, so it would reproduce successfully. Its first print run was 5,000—a delivery that coincided with the birth of her seventh child. The premiere issue sold out immediately.

All the children who were old enough pitched in to help on the publishing operation. Mary Leman Austin was only 12 when *Quilter's Newsletter* started, yet she took on a lot of the artwork and illustrations for her mother. In 1996, Bonnie retired and Mary took over as editor-in-chief. When asked if she always saw eye-to-eye with her mother, she laughed, explaining, "Mom was a great one for stick-

"Quiltmakers weren't looking at history books, they were making history with their quilts. The how-to books and the magazines were the history books. At the time, the publishers didn't think of it that way; it just was."

-Eileen Janke Trestain

ing with it until I saw it her way! That certainly could have caused conflict between a mother and her daughter, but looking back, I realize it was the best education she could have given me. Besides, even with the potential tensions of a mother-daughter working relationship, I always knew that my boss would love me at the end of the day."

Another early title—short-lived, but beloved—was *Nimble Needle Treasures* (NNT), a quarterly out of Oklahoma edited by Pat Almy. Celebrated quilter Dolores Hinson wrote for NNT, and she urged quilt historian Cuesta Benberry to do the same. The magazine went out of business in the mid-1970s. Produced in New York City, *Lady's Circle Patchwork Quilts* magazine was first published in 1973 as a quarterly, then expanded to six issues a year in 1985. Another bimonthly begun in the mid-1970s was *Quilt World*, from The House of White Birches, a publishing company in New Hampshire.

In 1984, avid quilt collectors Meredith and Bill Schroeder in Paducah, Kentucky, started the American Quilter's Society (AQS). Publishers since 1970 of collectors' price guides for antiques, they recognized that quilting was exploding in popularity and that American quilters truly were a society. In the same year, their quarterly magazine, *American Quilter*, began as a wonderful perk for AQS members, and Meredith was its first editor. Later, several other magazines devoted to quiltmaking started up and established their niche: *American Patchwork & Quilting*, *McCall's Quilting*, *Quilting Today*, and a magazine from Marianne Fons and Liz Porter, launched as *Sew Many Quilts*, later retitled *Fons & Porter's Love of Quilting*.

Meredith Schroeder, founder and president of the American Quilter's Society.
Photo by Charles Lynch.

Books

If you were a quilter in the early 1970s, books about your passion were rare. Those that did exist were highly valued. As the quilt revival took off, quilt-publishing houses emerged whose main focus was to produce quilt books. In 1976, former elementary school teacher Nancy J. Martin launched That Patchwork Place in the Seattle, Washington area, later to be called Martingale & Co. In 1983, with a Roberta Horton manuscript in hand, quilter Carolie Hensley and her husband, Tom Hensley, put their initials together to name their new company, C&T Publishing, Inc., located in the San Francisco area. And in 1985, the American Quilter's Society began publishing books in Paducah, Kentucky, along with the aforementioned *American Quilter* magazine. Other companies established large quilt-book divisions, such as Rodale Press and Oxmoor House.

Selected *Quilter's Newsletter* magazine covers from 1970.
Cover No. 11: courtesy of the Denver Art Museum.

Quilt Lovers, Unite!

"Because the generations of needlewomen on Mom's side never made a quilt and I knew no quilters, the Dover reprints of the Marguerite Ickis and Ruby Short McKim books were my only source of information."
-Dixie Haywood

Besides quilt-book publishers, organizations to nurture the growth of quilting were springing up in many pockets of America. In 1979, Hazel Carter started the Quilter's Hall of Fame (QHF), which has honored many pioneers and leaders who have made outstanding contributions to the world of quilting. For a long time the QHF existed without a real home. As Hazel says, "It was only on paper until my meeting in 1991 with the granddaughter of Marie Webster, who asked if I would like to house the organization in her grandmother's home in Marion, Indiana." Marie Webster was a famous quilt designer who operated a successful pattern business in the 1930s. Her work inspired renditions throughout the twentieth century. A slew of renovations have been readying the historic, colonial revival home where Marie Webster lived from 1902 to 1942 for its official opening in 2004.

In Mill Valley, California, in 1980, Sally Garoutte founded the American Quilt Study Group (AQSG). What began as a small group gathered around Sally's kitchen table led to the first AQSG seminar in the same year, then grew into a highly respected organization whose members preserve quilt heritage through research and publications, as well as the yearly seminars.

In 1981, The Kentucky Quilt Project, with Shelly Zegart as the driving force, was the first of the state quilt documentation projects that were (and continue to be) conducted all over the country. Calls went out for people to bring their family heirlooms in to be documented, and they came in droves. This created a groundswell for quilt appreciation, which spun out into quilt collecting, quilt conservation, quilt repair, the copying of historic quilts, and on into contemporary, innovative quiltmaking.

A few years later, thanks to movers and shakers from organizations and guilds, museums dedicated to quilts appeared. The year 1987 saw the founding of the New England Quilt Museum in Lowell, Massachusetts. In 1990, the Rocky Mountain Quilt Museum was founded in Golden, Colorado. In 1991, the Museum of the American Quilter's Society (MAQS) opened its doors in Paducah, Kentucky, and the Latimer Quilt & Textile Center began in Tillamook, Oregon. Then in 1997, the LaConner Quilt Museum of LaConner, Washington, sixty miles north of Seattle, joined the party.

Museum of the American Quilter's Society, Paducah, Kentucky.

The Alliance for American Quilts, founded in 1993 by Karey Bresenhan, Nancy O'Bryant, Shelly Zegart, and Eunice Ray, sought to unite the various elements of the quilt world, preserve its history, and advance quilt appreciation. Then in 1999, four major non-profit quilt organizations—The Alliance for American Quilts, American Quilt Study Group, International Quilt Association, and National Quilting Association—came together to conduct the Ultimate Quilt Search, sponsored by the International Quilt Festival, *Quilter's Newsletter Magazine*, *Quiltmaker*, and *McCall's Quilting*. These organizations and sponsors created a panel of distinguished experts to select the best one hundred quilts from the twentieth century. Many of the quilts shown in this book have received that special honor.

CONWAY ALBUM
(I'M NOT FROM BALTIMORE)
(90" x 90", 1992)
by Irma Gail Hatcher,
was selected as one of the
Twentieth Century's
100 Best American Quilts.
In the collection of the
Museum of the American Quilter's Society.

Celebrating Quilts: Festivals & Shows

In places around the country where several guilds were clustered, collective clout resulted in regional quilt shows and major quilt festivals. In 1976, the Bicentennial Finger Lakes Quilt Exhibit probably set the trend. Fifteen counties in upstate New York, led by the Tompkins Country Quilters Guild, collected more than 600 quilts to display in the Ithaca Senior High School. There were demonstrations and quilting bees for children as well as adults, and already famous authors and experts gave workshops and lectures. In 1977, the Lincoln (Nebraska) Quilters Guild sponsored Quilt Symposium '77, where Helen Squire presented history and folklore, Phyllis Haders lectured on old Amish quilts, and Michael James spoke on contemporary quilt art.

Also in the year 1977, Richard Cleveland found himself head of the Northfield Historical Society in Vermont. He wanted to put a few quilts in the front window of the historical society's building as part of the town's annual Labor Day celebration. Needing to augment the few old quilts that had been in his family, he asked around for contributions. Before he knew it, he had more than one hundred quilts to show. It was clear the exhibit had turned into something that wouldn't fit in that storefront window, so an armory was rented. The Vermont Quilt Festival (VQF) was born in that 1977 one-day exhibit at the armory. The next year, the Vermont Quilt Festival grew to two days, and the next year to three. By 1983, it had outgrown the armory and taken over the campus of a military college. "By 2000," Richard says, "the Vermont Quilt Festival was a huge operation that depended on four hundred volunteers a year, quite a lot of them members of local guilds."

Rita Barber, organizer of the Quilter's Heritage Celebration (QHC), tells a similar story. In 1983, she planned a regional quilt show to be held in Carlinville, Illinois, forty-five miles south of Springfield. "You have to have a quilting constituency and a network even if you do advertising," Rita says. "Once word got around that there might be a show, the local Red Rose Quilters guild pitched in to help." The first conference was the template for all that followed, and it included classes, lectures, dinners with a special speaker, an exhibit hall, and vendors. In June of that year, the first Quilter's Heritage Celebration went on as planned. "Within four years, we were drawing more than 5,400 participants, which was more than the population of the town," says Rita. "We were turning away a great number of people, so I looked for another site." She found it in the heart of Amish country—Lancaster, Pennsylvania. There, QHC grew from three days to four, and early-bird classes were added before opening day.

The One and Only Trade Show

Karey Bresenhan is well known and appreciated for advancing quiltmaking. The support of family and an active local quilting guild were key to her achievements. Karey is a fifth generation quilter. In 1974, she opened a Houston area quilt store called Great Expectations where her mother, Jewel Patterson, taught and worked. At the end of that first year, Karey and Jewel gave a

"I'm just home from one of our modern 'gathering of the clans,' that giant quilting bee, a quilt symposium.... No wonder I couldn't get to sleep after splashing all day in that great big bowl of quilt-borscht."

-Helen Kelley
From Quilter's Newsletter Magazine (1984)

"There are quilters who would get out of a hospital bed to go to the Vermont Quilt Festival. There may even be people who would leave home on their husband's birthday or a daughter's wedding day to go to the Vermont Quilt Festival ... the friendliness, ease, and fun make it like going home to the best reunion you've ever been to."

-Carter Houck
From Quilter's Newletter Magazine (1996)

thank-you party for their customers, which started an annual tradition known as Quilt Festival. In 1976, Karey organized Quilt Fair '76, sponsored by the Quilt Guild of Greater Houston, which Karey and Jewel had co-founded. This was only the beginning. Under Karey's direction, the first and only trade show for quilting, or Quilt Market as it is called, debuted in Houston, Texas, in 1979. That event literally turned the quilting community into an industry. It included 189 retailers and teachers, and galvanized the manufacturers of sewing machines, fabric, batting, thread, notions, and cutting and ironing supplies. This was not so much a trade show as a phenomenon, because, for the first time, quilt shop owners could come to one place and find all the resources they needed to stock their shops and all the information for running their businesses. Every year, Quilt Market expanded, and so did the quilting industry. In 1981, a spring edition was launched in San Francisco in addition to the regular fall Quilt Market in Houston and the continuing Quilt Festival for consumers. In 2000, Quilt Market included 450 retailers, 801 booths, 65 teachers, and 86 classes, lectures, and special events. As in the past, Karey herself welcomed the thousands of quilt shop owners who came and thereby helped turn quiltmaking into a fiscally powerful, continually growing industry.

Karey Bresenhan, president of Quilts, Inc., and founder/director of
International Quilt Market,
International Quilt Festival, and
Patchwork & Quilt Expo.
Photo by Haney-Whipple, courtesy of Quilts, Inc.

If Houston is the Mecca for quiltmakers, Paducah is their Paris. The American Quilter's Society show started there in 1985 and quickly became the largest consumer quilting show in the world. Quilting fever overtakes the entire town during this show when tens of thousands of quilters arrive each April. All the downtown businesses, even the gas stations and shoe stores, display quilts. Executive Show Director Bonnie Browning, who has been the show's organizer since 1994, explains how monetary prizes brought quilt designers into the artistic pantheon. "What AQS did for the quilt world was to offer substantial prize money for the quilt contest winners. In 1985, that was $10,000 for the single Best of Show award, and $26,000 in total prizes. By 2000, AQS was presenting more than $100,000 in cash awards. That put a value to quilts, a monetary value, like that of any other artwork." Quilting had truly arrived.

1987 American Quilter's Society quilt show.

Fabric Shops Close, Quilt Shops Open

In the late 1970s, many fabric stores went out of business. Unless a woman had unusual or very discriminating tastes, there was no need for her to sew. Purchased clothing and home decorating items were abundant in every price range. By the early 1980s, J.C. Penney, Montgomery Ward, and many other department stores had closed their fabric departments. Ironically, quilting had by this time really started to catch on and grow, and quilters had trouble finding appropriate fabric for their projects. As their knowledge base grew, consumers started to reject the polyester-cotton blends that didn't hold a crease and were hard to needle.

The growing demand for a lot of choices in 100 percent cotton fabric for quilting spawned the specialty quilt shops. These were little mom-and-pop (or, more likely, mom-without-the-pop) businesses. Very often, a quilter set up shop out of a strong desire to acquire stock that she wanted to use in her own work, and to establish a base for classes. This was certainly true of Harriet Hargrave. Growing up, she had disdained her mother's attempts to teach her hand quilting, but she loved the sewing machine. Harriet became an adult-education teacher of machine embroidery and machine appliqué, starting about 1978. Two years later, with her mother by her side, she opened Harriet's Treadle Arts, one of the first quilt stores in the Denver area and certainly among the first nationwide to specialize only in machine quilting, piecing, and appliqué. The growth of that store, from a 600-square-foot house with a couple hundred bolts of fabric to a 4,000-square-foot commercial space with over 3,000 bolts, makes it a stellar example of the growth of quilt shops all over country during the 1980s and 1990s. Quilt shops quickly became great places to go whenever a quilter needed resources: materials, tools, and the friendly advice and informative support they gave quilters provided a powerful advantage over chain stores that might price their fabric lower but fall short in customer service.

Classes & Workshops

"Professional quilting teacher" was an extremely rare career choice before the late 1970s. But as the number of quilters grew, so did their demand for knowledge. Within a decade, there arose a good-sized group of professional quilters and workshop leaders. This in turn had an impact on the quilt revival movement itself. Rita Barber, who hired quilting teachers for her quilt conferences, states, "The celebrity teacher rarely gets to be that way without having the necessary skills. Look at the impact the work of these individuals has had on the look of quilts, the use of fabric in quilts, and the techniques for putting them together. These experts bring amazing ideas to the greater quilting community, and transmit the excitement through books and lectures."

Soon quilters were able to combine in-depth classes with a vacation setting. One of the first of these programs was the Jinny Beyer Seminar on Hilton Head Island, South Carolina, first held in 1981, and continuing to this day. Others offered quilting classes amidst the bucolic peace of New York's Thousand Lakes or overlooking Puget Sound near Seattle. Soon there were far afield trips for quilters to Japan and Africa. Classes were taught on quilt cruises that sailed to Alaska, Australia, Ireland, and other exciting destinations.

"Whenever you see someone quilt, you learn something new. I want my students to think, 'If she can do it, I can,' and I always say to them, 'Look what you've done and what you can do.' A little competitive camaraderie spurs people on to improve their skills."

—Georgia Bonesteel

"In quilting workshops, the camaraderie and willingness to share helps us all to grow. Teachers show students what they're excited about, even before it's published and protected by copyright. If you share, you get other ideas back from everyone else, and pretty soon you've enhanced your original design. In fact, most of my books have been an outgrowth of what I do in my seminars."

—Jinny Beyer

Channeling the Medium: TV

Even if you couldn't find good classes in your area or afford a quilting vacation, you could still have someone show you how to make a quilt. Good classroom teachers, such as Jinny Beyer, made videos, and those who had a special flair and energy for teaching appeared on TV. In the early days of televised quilting lessons, you had to be prepared for the unexpected on the set.

In 1981, *Quilting* was the first TV series for quilters, broadcast from Bowling Green, Ohio, on WBGU-TV with Penny McMorris as its hostess. Much to everyone's surprise, fifty stations around the United States quickly signed up for the show. It was a thirteen-show series, which ran weekly. A series called *Quilting II* followed the next year. Then, in 1991, Penny produced another TV series, called *The Great American Quilt*. Getting great techniques in front of quilters was always a prime objective, even when there was little time for preparation. Penny laughed, remembering a program on which she shared the Electric Quilt, a computer software program her husband had finished creating only the night before. "I had never done more than look at it and really had no idea what I was doing," Penny says. "Though the camera never betrayed us, my husband was actually crouching behind the table, working the keyboard, operating the software, bringing the correct visuals up on the computer monitor, and cueing me. At the end, I looked straight at the camera and said, 'Now, wasn't that easy?' If viewers had only known ...."

Although most TV quilting shows feature the social interaction of the host and at least one guest, the shows that paired quilters Marianne Fons and Liz Porter reflect the special bond that many quilters have for each other. Marianne says, "Many quilters have a special quilt buddy they like to sew with. We get letters all the time from viewers who say they relate strongly to us because they have a quilting friend, too."

Penny McMorris
Quilting I, 1981; *Quilting II,* 1982;
The Great American Quilt, 1991.

Georgia Bonesteel
Lap Quilting with Georgia Bonesteel, 1982.

Marianne Fons and Liz Porter
Sew Many Quilts, 1995; *Quilting with Fons and Porter,* 1999
Photo by Craig Anderson.

Kaye Wood,
Strip Quilting, 1988,
Quilting for the '90s, 1991,
Kaye's Quilting Friends, 1995.
Photo by Kaye Wood, Inc.

Eleanor Burns,
Quilt in a Day, 1990.
Photo by Wayne Norton,
Norton Photography,
San Maros, CA.

Sharlene Jorgenson,
Quilting from the Heartland, 1992.
Photo by Jerry Klassen @ Lane Studio.

Alex Anderson,
Simply Quilts, 1997.
Photo courtesy of
Home & Garden Television.

Once upon a time in America, regional differences among quilters seemed to be in effect. The Midwest and New England were regarded as home for traditional piecing, the South prided itself on traditional appliqué, and California was a hotbed of fun and funky innovation. But then came traveling teachers, a good distribution of how-to books, national quilt shows, and, most effective of all, cable TV. With all this access to a diversity of techniques, quilters all over the U.S. became enlightened, empowered, and far more likely to break out of any regional stereotypes.

Enter the Internet

Social fulfillment and hands-on opportunities provided by guilds and classes were still not available to those quilters hampered by geographical isolation, full-time jobs, or family lives too hectic to allow for active guild participation. But by the end of the twentieth century, quilters had another way of sharing with each other: the Internet.

According to Gloria Hansen, the first services that catered to quilters with computer bulletin boards were early commercial services, such as GEnie (General Electric Network for Information Exchange), Prodigy, and Delphi. Gloria was an early member of the GEnie Online Quilters group, which she joined in 1991. GEnie offered a bulletin board with several categories, a library, and conference rooms where quilters could chat with each other. Topics posted on bulletin boards allowed quilters to share techniques, exchange blocks and fabric, and issue and exhibit challenges.

This alternative way of connecting with other quilters was far from impersonal. As Gloria acclaims, appropriately enough in an e-mail: "Quilters regularly supported each other. They'd rejoice when awards were won, console when rejections were received, offer advice when someone hit a creative void." Even more, they cried at family deaths, supported one another during illnesses, and stitched quilts to console quilters who'd lost their life's work to fire or flood.

As the World Wide Web grew by leaps and bounds, services that provided text-based bulletin boards faded away. In 1999, GEnie changed its services, and the GEnie Online Quilters was no more. After 1999, most quilters who subscribed to online services either migrated to the quilting area of America Online or ventured directly to the World Wide Web.

But even those quilters who no longer participated in online quilting groups—or never did—enjoyed friendships and shared information via e-mail. Web-surfers scouted and shared advice and patterns. Quiltmakers proudly gave Show 'n Tells of their latest works, just like at a guild meeting or a solo exhibition at a quilt show, but this time, viewers admired digital or scanned images at a site in cyberspace. Teachers promoted their lectures and workshops on Web sites, connecting with guilds and scoring teaching jobs.

The Quilting in America™ 2000 survey, sponsored by Primedia and Quilts, Inc., pointed out the changes since the 1997 survey, proclaiming "a real upswing in the presence of computers and the Internet in quilters' lives. A total

"The Internet has connected the world into a vast, virtual quilting bee, available whenever we are willing to tap into it. I'm a frequent attendee, often in the wee hours of the night while I'm in my PJs!"

-Gloria Hansen

of 76 percent of dedicated quilters—those who devote the most time and money to their craft—own computers (up 15 percent from 1997), and 57 percent of them log on every day. The average dedicated quilter also spends 2.1 hours each week visiting strictly quilt-related Web sites. Primary reasons include: to find out about quilting products, learn new tips and techniques, and receive free quilt or block patterns."

A Family Tree of Quilters

Deeply rooted in historical tradition, quiltmaking managed to work its roots into the very souls of its participants and devotees. During the '70s, '80s, and '90s, it grew to mammoth proportions, branching off in a hundred directions.

Quiltmaking was always a family tree in America, one with a strong support system that nourished creativity and brought personal expression into flower. Naturally, there were always quilters who worked and developed entirely on their own, but quilting flourished when it stayed close to its roots as a social tradition, in a gathering of two people or two thousand. When skills and information were shared, real enthusiasm blossomed.

CYBER CONNECTION
(87½" x 87½", 2000) by Carol Taylor.
Photo by the artist.

JOURNEY THROUGH TIME
(68" x 68", 1991) by Suzanne Marshall.
Photo by Red Elf.

The Fabric Explosion:
Ultimate Inspiration

At the beginning of the 1970s, most of the fabrics on the market were polyester (a lot of stretchy double-knits), polyester-cotton, or rayon. Lacking know-how, a novice quilter often chose to put together scraps of these fabrics from various clothing projects. Minnie Loeper, for example, used a wide assortment of synthetics to make a quilt for her daughter, who was getting married. Completed in 1976, the gift was heartfelt and offered many fond memories of what the family had worn, but it weighed a ton, and many areas of the surface tended to stretch and pill (see page 32).

Even experienced quilters had to make do with a small selection of 100 percent cotton dress-weight goods offered by a handful of companies. "We didn't call it 100 percent cotton, let alone quilter's cotton back then. We called it 'real' cotton," says longtime quilter and historian Judy Roche. Thirty years later, however, the fabric scene had completely changed. There were thousands of "quilter's cottons," with new collections pouring out

HELIACAL RISE (74" x 71", 1996)
by Laura Murray.
In the collection of the
Museum of the American Quilter' Society.

Detail of Minnie Loeper's wedding gift quilt, made by using a variety of synthetic fabrics.
Photo by John P. Hamel.

"Oh, the wrinkles you had to contend with for any clothing that was 100 percent cotton. Remember putting wet, cotton shirts in the freezer, and ironing them right after taking them out? Most of us were delighted to have poly-cotton instead for our garments. But for quilting, we wanted cotton, and yet nineteenth-century people on the prairie had more choices of 100 percent cotton than we did in 1970."

-Marti Michell

twice a year from nearly one hundred fabric companies. Head over heels in love with fabric, the quilting community couldn't (and still can't!) get enough.

Taking a Cotton to Cotton

"Quilters couldn't be good customers-they only wanted three-inch pieces." That was the prevailing opinion among fabric companies. The desired customer was the one buying five yards at a time to make a dress.

In the late 1960s and early 1970s, Marti Michell was instrumental in taking the market for cotton fabrics from poor to plentiful. She taught quilting classes, and she preached the superiority of 100 percent cotton for quilting. Marti didn't want to send her quilting students all over town to find cottons, so she put together kits containing cotton fabrics, which she got straight from the fabric companies. Under the name Yours Truly, Marti's company was buying substantial amounts of yardage, and one fabric mogul took notice. When Leo Driscoll, the president of V.I.P. Fabrics, asked Marti, "Could you tell me one more time why you want 100 percent cotton fabric?" she explained it all, just as quilting teachers explain it to their students: Wrinkle resistance is a detraction; for seams and appliqués to lie flat, fabric has to hold a crease. Silkiness is not a plus; slippery fabrics are a hassle to control. Neither is ultra-durability a good thing. Quilting fabrics are most desirable if they are soft and have just a little ease, or stretchiness, so they are easy to needle. Marti must have done a good job convincing this supplier, because he had been ready to drop all the 100 percent cottons in favor of poly-cotton blends. Instead, he kept cottons in his line.

V.I.P. was the leading company in cotton fabric at that time. Cranston was also on the scene, soon followed by Concord. Hoffman also offered 100 percent cotton screen prints, but these were primarily used to make Hawaiian shirts, mostly sold in Hawaii, and at that time, just a small part of the business. As a handful of companies began to pay attention to the cry for cotton, world events seemed to favor quiltmakers. Petroleum-based polyester lost a little of its glow during the winter of '73-'74, when an oil crisis in the Middle East made oil prices soar. (Many quilters remember waiting in long lines at the gas stations!) Coincidentally, at that time, China began to export huge amounts of cotton fabric, and fabric companies began to convert the goods into a multitude of coordinated calico prints.

Marti Michell explains, "In 1972, if you scoured every company for all-cotton fabric, as I did, it was hard to find 100 different bolts. By the time people started saying, 'I don't think I want to do kits, I want to find my own fabric'—and this was 1977 or 1978—it was easy to find a store that carried 500 to 700 different bolts of cotton."

Progress in Production

From the late 1970s through the mid 1980s, the number of companies producing 100 percent cotton expanded. Springs Industries, Peter Pan, Ameritex, and Wamsutta were all manufacturing this product, but for them quilting fabric remained a sideline, a mere add-on, but not the dominant part of their businesses. Benartex, P&B, R.J.R. Fabrics, and South Seas joined the ranks, at first operating in the same way as their competitors, but eventually moving into all-cotton merchandise. These companies started as distributors, buying the finished goods (fabrics). Later, they all became converters—buying the raw goods but taking control over the dyeing, printing, and finishing. In the beginning, the basic fabric, or greige (pronounced "gray") goods was produced domestically. But economic and regulatory issues made it more cost efficient to buy greige goods from various international suppliers, mostly in China, India, and other parts of Asia.

How and where dyeing and printing were done changed as well. Here in the U.S., each screen printing or application of a single color was very costly, and consequently, any given fabric design was kept to just a few colors. Furthermore, the Environmental Protection Agency limited the use of certain dyes. So, to avoid regulations, offer multicolor prints, and still keep fabric prices attractive to quilters, companies began to have cotton fabrics printed, as well as woven, overseas. This way, they could avail themselves of the newest fiber-reactive dyes. Printed fabrics were less likely to "crock" (in which the dye rubs off), bleed, or quickly fade. Selim Benardette, the president of Benartex Fabrics, fondly known in the business as Mr. B., explains, "As technology improved, the detail and number of colors that you could put on the greige goods improved enormously. By the 1990s, the better fabrics might have 15 to 18 different screens, with a real clarity of detail and depth of color."

But that wasn't all. Fabrics became more finely and evenly woven, which meant raw edges wouldn't fray as easily and batting fibers were less likely to poke their way through the weave. Finishing agents as well as the tighter weaves, helped decrease fabric shrinkage.

The increasing quality thrilled the quilters, and their purchasing power encouraged many businesses to turn exclusively to the quilting market and to make quilting cotton their only product. Benartex was one such company in the late '80s. Mr. B. takes pride in how his business caters to the quilter. At the same time, he attests to the merits of healthy competition. "Overall, the quality is excellent, and it's not only us. We are really motivated by the work of our wonderful competitors."

"The first quilt shop in my area opened in the late 1970s with some of the most wonderful prints for quilting. I threw out all my clothing patterns, because who wants to make blouses using one fabric apiece when you can make a quilt and get to work with all these great fabrics?"
-Diane Gaudynski

The Rise of Commercial Fabrics

Inevitably, improved fabric quality, along with inflation, led to increased prices. Prices were usually a little lower in the chain stores, but sometimes the greige goods used for the chains were of a lesser quality, or the designs were a little less complex. Expert quilters reminded their sister consumers, "You get what you pay for." Independent quilt shops, called "indies" in the trade, quickly became more competitive and business savvy, offering special sales and promotions regularly. Nonetheless, it was only natural that most quilters sought the cheapest prices they could find. Lower prices at chain stores such as JoAnn's, Hancock, and Wal-Mart stores were an ever-appealing lure.

To compete for the quilt customer, every indie offset its higher prices with service. The woman behind the quilt shop counter was invariably knowledgeable about fabric and understood that it was her job to guide customers in making wise purchasing decisions. By contrast, the sales staff at the chains, if you could find someone to help you, was less likely to be able to educate or assist the customer in these critical areas.

Understanding the importance of quilters to their bottom line and knowing that quilt shops were a major pipeline to that customer, fabric companies supported the indies in many ways. Some companies committed to sell only to indies. They spent a lot of time with the buyer from an indie at the annual Quilt Market. They showed quilts made up with the new fabric collections, giving away the instructions so stores could make up their own samples. In between trade shows, they kept the quilt shops informed via mail and e-mail. And they employed good regional salespeople, each of whom cultivated relationships with the shops in his or her area, visiting them bimonthly or quarterly.

"Fran and I love to watch the reactions of people when they see my pants for the first time. They make people smile. They're a great way to meet people. Believe it or not, these crazy pants have enriched our lives."
-Dan Boltz

Dan, in loud pants, surrounded
by other pairs.
Photo by Richard H. Batchelor.

Dan's Pants

One of those salespeople was a legend in his own time. Six feet six inches tall, Dan Boltz literally towered above everyone else. Though he happened to have the perfect last name for a guy who sold bolts of fabric to quilt shops, he was often referred to as "Dan the Fabric Man." Dan worked as a sales representative for Concord Fabrics for 16 years, then for Hoffman Fabrics for 21 years. In 1984, his wife made him a pair of trousers from a Madras plaid he fancied. They were so comfortable, especially for traveling, that, before long, his closet was full of Fran's custom-made pants. Every season, Dan and Fran would select the most vibrant, eye-popping print to cover Dan's long legs. To be chosen, a fabric had to pass the "across the street test." If it wasn't noticeable from that distance, it didn't make the cut. Dan's pants made him a celebrity at Quilt Market and with quilt groups that booked Dan's trunk-show presentation. Quilters were always delighted by this huge guy and his outlandish pants.

The Hoffman Quilting Contest

Also originating from Hoffman Fabrics was the Hoffman Challenge, a contest that got its start in 1987 at the National Quilting Association (NQA) Show. Betty Boyink, of Betty Boyink Publishing, showed fellow exhibitor Holice Turnbow, of The Stencil Company, a particularly unusual fabric, and he promptly challenged her to use it in a quilt. At the well-attended Show 'n Tell, they extended the challenge to others. Quilting magazines spread the word even further, and by the time the 1988 NQA show rolled around, there were ninety-four entries. Betty and Holice continued to organize the Hoffman Challenge for many years. The contest and show continue to this day, organized by Hoffman staff.

Celebrity Designers

A new twist—printing the name of a well-known quilt artist or quilt-shop owner along the edges of fabric yardage—was another major boon for the indie quilt shops. The imprimatur of a renowned quilt designer, teacher, or historian quickly came to be a magnet for quiltmakers seeking new and interesting quality fabrics. They knew that celebrity designers were far more likely to understand the end use of the fabric than other fabric designers with artistic but not necessarily quilting talents.

The first star signature on the selvages was Jinny Beyer. A world-class quiltmaker, Jinny first came to fame in 1978, when her RAY OF LIGHT medallion quilt (see the photo on the cover and on page 66) won the top prize in the Great American Quilt Contest, sponsored by *Good Housekeeping* magazine and the U.S. Historical Society. Jinny tried to interest fabric companies in her fabric designs, but without success. Then she got help from two

"Most of my fabrics are now by designers, quilt artists, and very often quilt shop owners who really understand what quilters want and need. I like to call my lines, 'Fabric for Quilters, by Quilters."
—Selim Benardette (Mr. B.)

1998   1990   1992   1994   1995   1998   1999

A selection of Hoffman Challenge fabrics.

Fabrics from Jinny Beyer's
first collection.

*"Painters have to rely on brush strokes or
paper quality to create texture. But quilters
have visual texture built right into the beautiful fabrics we use ... I make my quilts from
printed fabric exclusively, and the interaction between different prints creates many
wonderful effects impossible to achieve with
paint or solid-colored fabrics."*

-Judy B. Dales

major forces in the quilting world. As
Jinny tells it, "Karey Bresenhan and
Nancy Puentes (Karey's cousin) were
always trying to help the quilt shops
compete with the chain stores' low
prices. They got the idea that a company should do a line of fabrics that
would only be available to the quilt
shops."

V.I.P. agreed to do it, and the first
Jinny Beyer collection was born in
1981. Of her start as a fabric designer,
she says, "I tried the front door and it
didn't work, so I went in the back
door." This first designer collection
included a border print, a coordinating large-scale, multi-color paisley
print, and a small-scale print. These
designs came in three different colorways: browns and rust; blues and bur-
gundy; and a red, green, and gold
palette. In 1984, R.J.R. Fabrics began producing Jinny's fabric collections.

From the beginning, Jinny's fabrics were unlike any others. "My husband
and I lived in Nepal, India, and Sarawak, Malaysia, which affected my sense
of colors and design. I loved looking at block prints, which often had borders along the selvages. I certainly felt the influence. Some people thought
my quilts looked like oriental rugs." To this day, Jinny Beyer's fabrics often
suggest a rich, Asian feeling, and always make a big impact on the quilting
industry.

When Jinny's designs first appeared, they opened quilters' eyes to fabric
design possibilities beyond those presented by small-scaled calicoes. The
success of fabrics with special name recognition for quilters led every company to seek out quilting celebrities to design fabrics. In the 1980s, many
fabrics bore the names of popular authors and teachers, such as Jeff
Gutcheon, Diana Leone, and Roberta Horton. In the '90s, the fabric designer scene positively exploded, and shows no sign of abating. Some celebrities
were illustrators, such as Debbie Mumm and Patrick Lose. Some, such as
Paul Pilgrim, Gerald Roy, Elly Sienkiewicz, and Barbara Brackman, were his-
torians, bringing an authenticity to quilter's cottons. And fabric collections
from well-known quilt artists, like Paula Nadelstern and Nancy Crow, nearly
guaranteed a jazzy, contemporary quilt.

Darlene Zimmerman, who put together the "Granny's" collections of '30s
reproduction fabrics for Jaftex/Chanteclaire, remembers a time before
designers got involved. "You really had to shop around and try to find all

the fabrics and get them to work together. Once designers coordinated collections, the quilter was relieved of a daunting responsibility." Since that time, the quilter can simply go to one collection, in the color palette of her choice, pick out a focus fabric, its coordinates in variously scaled patterns, the matching backgrounds, and the border stripes. In this way, she is certain of having the necessary variety of light-, medium-, and dark-color tone, and a pleasing balance of color, assuring success for her quilt project.

Fabric Trends

In the 1970s, traditional style dominated decorating and quiltmaking, and Williamsburg blue was one of the few alternatives to the crayon-bright intensity of most fabrics. A typical quilt at this time featured a pieced or appliquéd design, made from a couple of matching prints and a coordinating solid or two from among the few colors that were available. Almost invariably, the prints were tiny floral calicoes, and the background was a white or unbleached muslin.

In the 1980s, colors softened. Popular palettes included dusty pinks with cranberry. Earth tones were also popular. Viney florals spaced out along the background, often from Jinny Beyer, were a welcome change from the busy calico prints, and pin-dots were a fresh alternative to solids. Stripes and border prints were favored, and quilters began combining florals and directionals, though they were generally still timid about combining stripes and plaids. However, scrap quilts, which combined many prints for a rustic, country look, were very popular, and charm quilts with every piece in a different fabric were also admired and emulated.

In the 1990s, with the expanding choices of fabrics, quilts showcased subtle and sophisticated shifts of color, or a full spectrum of jewel tones. A background was just as likely to be a quiet print as a solid color. Quilters varied color values and visual textures, with help from fabric and quilt designers, quilt teachers, authors, and quilt shop staffers. Dots were hot, and jazzy geometrics began to enliven quilts of all kinds. Nature prints were new in the '90s, and continue to be a natural choice, with rocks, wood, grass, tree bark, animal skins, sky, and water.

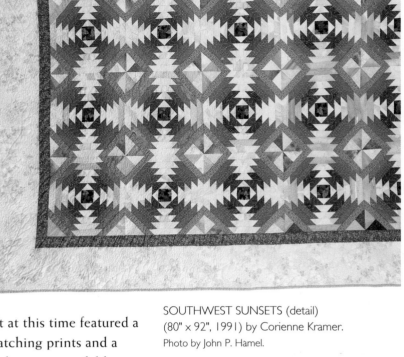

SOUTHWEST SUNSETS (detail)
(80" x 92", 1991) by Corienne Kramer.
Photo by John P. Hamel.

Georgia Bonesteel shows off her Drunkard's Path quilt in a 1970's class.

Popular Patterns: Repros and Pictorials

Certain categories of patterned fabrics first achieved great popularity in the 1990s. Probably the best-selling genre was, and still is, "repro" fabric, reproductions of antique or vintage fabrics. According to fabric historian Eileen Jahnke Trestain, repros really began to take off in 1993 and 1994, "People were seeing old quilts in museums and historical societies. And Civil War re-enactors sparked an interest in authentic looks, such as the Dear Jane® patchwork." (See page 64 to read about the 1863 quilt that launched this nostalgic passion.) The biggest collections of reproduction fabrics targeted the antebellum era and the period from 1880 to 1900. Depression era or 1930s fabrics, from quilts, clothing, and feed sacks, also inspired a wealth of reproduction fabrics. Even the '40s, '50s, and '60s were revisited with oversized florals, tea-dyed and faded looks, and textural barkcloth tropicals. If anyone lacked for quilts from her ancestors or antique dealers, she now had the means to create her own "heirloom."

Conversation prints were another huge fabric revival. Small-scale, pictorial novelty prints were not new, but each year since the late 1980s brought motifs that were fresher, funkier, or sweeter than before. Quilters used these little prints to echo a theme: a tiny sailboat or celestial print for a Mariner's Compass pattern, a goose print in a Wild Goose Chase design. One popular way quilters spotlighted their favorite print motifs was with an "I Spy" quilt, in which a small figure or item on a printed fabric was centered inside each

Nature prints were new in the '90s.

These florals, all manufactured in the 1990s, reproduce fabrics from the early 1800s up to the 1950s.

patch. Starting in 1991, Pat Yamin, who wrote *Look What I See Quilts*, designed and manufactured acrylic templates in many shapes.

On the opposite end of the spectrum from small-sized prints were the super-sized prints. Large scenes and still lifes were perfect for a medallion quilt, an attic windows design, or simply to add interest to large plain blocks. Giant pictorials brought eye-popping whimsy to juvenile prints, making the simplest crib quilt, security blanket, or dorm quilt a very appreciated gift. Nancy Crow, Roberta Horton, Libby Lehman, and other quilt artists urged students in workshops to bring in the big scale, and kick up-or kick out-the little calicoes.

MILLENNIUM JELLYBEAN, (detail).

MILLENNIUM JELLYBEAN (56" x 72", 1999) by Ami Simms.
Ami used a variety of conversation prints collected through the
'90s in this "I Spy" type of quilt.
Photo by Axis Creative Group, Troy, Michigan.

Roberta Horton in 1982, in front of
WINGED UNDERCURRENTS (43" × 50",
1982), a quilt with large-scale prints.
Photo by Sharon Risedorph.

Yikes, Stripes! and Mad for Plaid

During every era, there have always been directional patterns: stripes, plaids, and ginghams. In the three decades at the end of the twentieth century, fabric companies kept directionals as mainstays, and quilters explored the versatility of these fabrics to the max. They adopted them all: humble homespun with the pattern woven in; prints ranging from ornate serpentine stripes to wild joyrides of racy curves; and border stripes, inspiring countless blocks and medallions, in addition to sashings and borders. Quilters cut along, across, and diagonal to stripes in their fabrics, creating all sorts of special effects.

Mary Mashuta, a quilt designer and teacher since 1985, frequently said, "I love stripes and have been including them in my garments forever and in my quilts for years." Mary was most likely to utilize a stripe cut strictly along the grain. On the other hand, her twin sister, Roberta Horton, was more apt to cut her striped and plaid fabrics "casually off-grain" for a scrappy look. Roberta's fabric designs included homespun and ikat, with threads dyed in contrast-color intervals and woven to form complex directional patterns.

TOURIST IN THE GOURMET GHETTO
(59½" × 59½", 1994)
by Mary Mashuta.
Photo by Sharon Risedorph.

Mary Mashuta shows her stripes
in this photo from 1989.
Photo by Sharon Risedorph.

In the late 1990s, needlework designer Kaffe Fassett took a love of stripes even further. Inspired by the Madras stripes of the '50s and '60s, this American, who has spent much of his life in England, decided to devote his attention to a Madras-style collection. Production of this fabric threw an economic lifeline to a tiny remote village in India where the fabrics were hand-woven from hand-dyed threads. The resulting fabric was unique in weight and texture, quite unlike the smooth, almost perfect commercial fabrics more typical of recent times. Kaffe's designs showed how the occasional glitch could add character to a finished quilt.

Global Influences

In the economic boom of the '80s and '90s, many Americans had the means for leisure trips, and quilters who traveled often took time out to shop for fabric. Even stores in other parts of the U.S. opened up new worlds of fabric. Quilts made of fabrics not seen in local quilt shops were more likely to catch the attention of local quilting buddies, generating envious expressions of, "Where did you get that fabric?"

Fabrics from the Far East beckoned. Beginning as early as the late 1970s, historic Japanese textiles were of special interest to Americans. Imported yukata and kimono hand-dyed cotton fabrics gained a following despite their narrow fourteen-inch widths. In the 1980s, Kasuri Dyeworks in Berkeley, California, and Quilter's Express in New York City made indigo a cool commodity. Shibori, a Japanese dye-resist process, influenced American quilt artists to adopt similar techniques for dyeing fabrics to create streaked and circular designs. Fabric companies large and small featured hand-dyed fabrics, often with batik and woodblock motifs, from Bali, Java, and Malaysia. Producing and importing these special fabrics made them expensive, but many a quilter splurged on a small piece. On rare occasions, a quilt shop or a booth at a show offered Australian fabrics, inspired by Aboriginal art; Mexican and Guatemalan fabrics, riotous with color; and Dutch treats with sophisticated colors and elegant motifs.

Stripes and plaids from the Kaffe Fassett collection.

DREAMS OF AFRICA
(40" x 35", 1996)
by Carole Lyles Shaw.

In the 1990s, African fabrics started showing up in quilt-show booths and quickly found a following. Mudcloth; Kuba cloth; African batiks, such as adire cloth from Nigeria; and fabrics printed with masks, elephants, wild cats, and snakes, imparted a bold and exciting look. African-American quilt artists often called upon these fabrics to express a side of their identity. Explaining the batik fabric used in her 1996 art quilt DREAMS OF AFRICA, Carole Lyles Shaw said, "Many years ago, I bought this batik because I recognized the African man in the fabric as a brother. When I saw it, my spirit felt as if it were being called home."

International fabrics available in the '90s.

In the 1990s, American fabric companies, such as Timeless Treasures and P&B Fabrics, began producing collections inspired by African and Japanese fabrics. Authors and quilt teachers, like Roberta Horton, Mary Mashuta, and Kaye England, promoted both authentic and international-styled fabrics in their books, workshops, and quilting tours. Other artists showed eclectic combinations of global fabrics and unusual textures that turned even a traditional pattern on its ear. One such artist is Laura Murray. Her award-winning HELI-ACAL RISE (1996) features Mexican and Thai ikat cottons for the Mariner's Compass points, African mudcloth for the border, along with silk charmeuse from China for accents, and Laura's own hand-dyed fabrics for the background. (See the cover and page 31.)

The Texture Revival

In the early 1980s, fabrics that had the same glossy luster as eighteenth- and nineteenth-century English chintz arrived, to the delight of quilters, particularly contemporary artists. Among those manufacturing these fabrics was Jeffrey Gutcheon of Gutcheon Patchworks in New York City. "Shimmery Solids! New! Polished 100 percent cottons— 35 colors!" crowed a 1982 ad from Cabin Fever Calicoes, which, despite its name, specialized in solid fabrics.

ARABIC #1 (64" x 80").
Polished cottons give this 1981 quilt by Sonya Lee Barrington its sheen.
Photo by Elaine Keenan Photography.

In the late 1990s, rustic homespun became a key ingredient for folk-art quilts, and flannel was just beginning to work its warm and fuzzy way into quilters' hearts. More experienced quilters, who had already learned the basics of using easy-to-handle cottons, often turned to fancier fabrics as their work progressed. Inspired by Victorian crazy quilts, they incorporated velvets and velveteens, organdy, satin, silk, lace, taffeta, brocade, and even tapestry fabrics in their quilts. Textural variety is now a fact of life, in the marketplace and in our quilts.

Hand-Dyed Fabrics

Quiltmakers seeking to simulate the Amish look, achieve a bold and contemporary look, introduce the illusion of dimension, or capture the colors of nature in their quilts craved many more fabric colors than the marketplace provided. To solve this problem, many quilters took up dyeing their own fabrics. Those who developed a real proficiency, like Jan Myers Newberry and Debra Lunn, taught and wrote about their techniques and often made hand-dyeing fabrics a business.

Beth Cassidy took a class with Debra Lunn and was inspired to start Alaska Dyeworks, in 1988, with Susan Roberts. They began dyeing two-yard pieces of cotton in buckets to achieve the progression of colors Beth needed for her quilt landscapes to create an illusion of depth and dimension. Said Victoria Barnett, who took over the business in May 1992, "There are parts of the country with great natural beauty, and many fiber artists wanted to capture that. This is especially true in Alaska."

"I began dyeing my own fabrics in 1984, for my own work, but, of course, you always end up dyeing a lot more fabric than you could ever use yourself, so I started selling it in 1995."

-Caryl Bryer Fallert

Alaska Dyeworks' most popular product combines many colors of the Alaskan landscape.

Many companies producing hand-dyed fabrics came and went during the '80s and '90s. Along with Alaska Dyeworks, the ones with staying power and great popularity included Cherrywood Fabrics and Primrose Gradations. In addition, several recognized artists began selling their hand-dyed cottons and sometimes silk fabrics and threads as well: Sonya Lee Barrington, Melody Johnson and Laura Wasilowski of Artfabrik, Mickey Lawler of Skydyes, and Caryl Bryer Fallert.

The Shelf Life of Fabrics

Quilt shop owners have always felt enormous pressure to have a lot of new fabric on hand every time their regular customers come in. Former quilt shop owner Cyndi Hershey states a business truism, "A quilt shop either has to grow or go." Limited shelf space meant that inventory had to move quickly. Consequently fabric companies printed small runs of more fabrics. When they ran out, that was it. Reprinting was seldom done.

In a 1992 issue of *Quilter's Newsletter Magazine*, columnist Jeffrey Gutcheon pointed out, "Without question, shop owners love every piece of fabric they buy, or they wouldn't buy it. But waiting for their customers to agree can be ruinous. The useful shelf life of fabric is nine months at best."

Given such retail realities, quilters were often up the creek if they found themselves short of a particular fabric for that quilt they had started six months before. All too often, they would find that wonderful tone-on-tone was no longer available. It was a rare happening when a fabric was such a good seller that a company kept it in their line for a long time. One of these exceptions to the one-season rule was Fossil Fern, designed by Patricia Campbell for Benartex in 1996. Quite possibly the best-selling fabric design of all time, it is still being reprinted.

Another problem with fabric inventory was that, by the time a great quilt appeared in a magazine or book, the fabrics it showcased (and which most readers specifically wanted) were no longer available. Jinny Beyer met this challenge head on with her new Macintosh computer in the early '90s. "I would scan the new fabrics into my computer and plug them, in the correct proportional scale, into a quilt design on the computer. We'd make this virtual quilt available just as the fabrics arrived in the shops."

Benartex's wildly successful Fossil Fern in a few colorways.

Lynette Jensen, designing under the Thimbleberries® name, also surmounted timing difficulties by coordinating on-sale dates for her quilt designs with the necessary fabrics. Thus, the Thimbleberries customer had a fail-proof guide to a well-designed quilt, with patterns and directions, complete with a specific designation of fabric for each section of the quilt.

Millennium Fabrics

While most top-selling fabrics had a timeless look about them, others had good timing going for them. Just as the bicentennial-inspired quilts that sang "Happy Birthday" to our country, the Y2K party for the millennium was an invitation to bellow "Happy New Year" with commemorative quilts galore. Many fabric companies were delighted to help quilters ring in the new millennium by incorporating fabric with the repeat-motif "2000," and hundreds of

An assortment of Millennium fabrics.

contests and challenges encouraged quilters to use these fabrics in traditional or contemporary designs. Including a commemorative fabric was one way to mark the date of one's quilt, which, together with a signed label, would make it more valuable as an heirloom and legacy.

Kits and Cuts

Many quilters found the enormous selection of fabrics intimidating. Beginners or busy quilters wanted to spend their time and money on a sure thing. For these people, kits were an easy sale throughout the '70s, '80s, and '90s. A kit contained a photo of a finished quilt, patterns, directions, and sometimes fabric. Quilt shops made up samples and hung them on the walls. A customer could admire the sample she saw on the shop wall, knowing she could produce the same quilt.

Most kits did not include fabric, enabling the consumer to substitute her own color and fabric preferences. In the '70s and early '80s, a quilter had to buy yardage, and most stores had a minimum amount they would cut, which was at

Quilt shops found many appealing ways to turn fat quarters into eye candy.

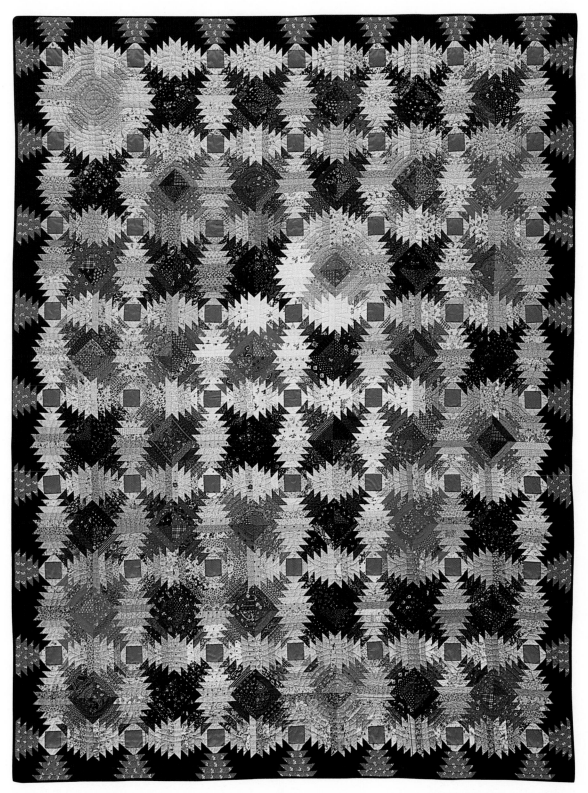

least a quarter yard, and sometimes a half yard. By the early 1990s though, most quilt shops were cutting fabric from the bolt to create fat quarters, pieces 18" x 22", and fat eighths, 9" x 22". Such "quilter's candy" made an appealing impulse buy and helped the quilter fill in the gaps for a project that required a lot of different fabrics.

MEMORIES (63" x 81", 1988).
Dixie Haywood used cotton scraps she'd collected from many years of quilting.
Photo by Greg Plachta.

Free Choice

In the 1990s, many handy helps became available to quilters who wanted to choose their own fabrics for a quilt. Suddenly, there were books and teachers offering quilters exercises in color and design.

Shops and catalogs began stocking gadgets, like carry-along color wheels, with windows for locating color complements and coordinates, and value finders made of transparent red acrylic, which made everything look rosy, so one could focus solely on the relative contrast of values. The end of the century also provided the high-tech end of the spectrum. New quilting software let the computer user download actual fabrics and audition them in a quilt design.

Managing One's "Stash"

Those women who made the shift from garment making to quiltmaking were likely to keep their fabrics in the bottom drawer of a dresser or in boxes stored under the bed. Once the hobby became a passion, the quilter faced the need for more space for her stash of yardage, fat quarters, and scraps. The old chestnut, "You can never be too thin or too rich," was exchanged for the adages, "You can never have enough fabric" and "The one who dies with the most fabric wins."

New, ventilated shelving was available, which could hold fabric for several lifetimes' worth of quilts, all of it visible at a glance. Some dedicated quilters renamed the guest room "the sewing room," while quilt artists called the sewing room "the quilting studio." With only a modicum of guilt, designers and teachers admitted building additions for these studios, including plenty of space for their giant collections of fabric.

Karen Kay Buckley in her favorite spot.
Photo by Joseph D. Buckley.

Piecing Our Quilts: Precision, Pronto!

Patchwork Passion

To most of us, the typical American quilt is, and always has been, a patchwork bedcover, "patchwork" meaning pieced together, despite the use of the term to describe appliqué in earlier decades. Piecework involves an investment of time, money, and energy. "A" is for accuracy—in cutting, sewing, and pressing. To "arrive" is to join the pantheon of quilters who can fit together the geometric puzzle of sharp points, crisp intersections, and smooth curves. Beginners and experienced quiltmakers devote immeasurable time and care to the pursuit of perfect piecing and seek out the newest classes, techniques, and products to help them attain it. But quiltmakers know it's all worth it, for the pure satisfaction that results.

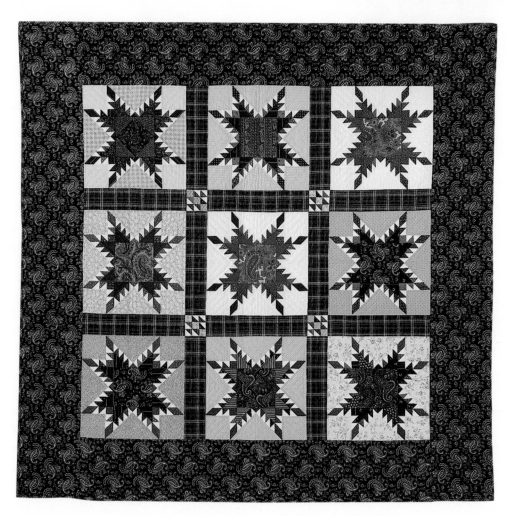

STAR OF CHAMBLIE (67" x 67", 1986)
by Marsha McCloskey.
In the collection of the
Museum of the American Quilter's Society.

"When avid quiltmakers confess to spending hundreds of hours working on a single quilt, eyebrows always go up. I'm sure folks imagine us hunched over needle and thread surrounded by neglected family members pleading for food, clean laundry, attention, love and companionship. Non-quilters must wonder what kind of idiot would spend that kind of time cutting cloth into pieces just to sew it together again when a great variety of suitable bedcovers are offered for sale at almost any department store."

-Ami Simms, 1985
- from How Not to Make a Prize-Winning Quilt

New Templates for the Times

In the early 1970s, we used templates cut from shirt cardboard or cereal boxes. Some clever quiltmakers made templates out of sandpaper, which would grip the fabric while you traced around it. The first plastic templates for piecing

were the brainchild of Bonnie Leman. Before she started *Quilter's Newsletter* in 1969 (later to become *Quilter's Newsletter Magazine*), Bonnie had a mail-order business selling her mother's old *Kansas City Star* quilt patterns, which she had traced and redrafted onto thin translucent plastic. Her husband, George, cut the patterns into squares and triangles with a paper cutter. Unlike cardboard, these plastic templates lasted through any project, allowing a quiltmaker to mark around them and transfer patch shapes for thousands of pieces. The translucency also made it possible and inviting to showcase a fabric motif on a patch. By the end of the twentieth century, template plastic in sheet form was a staple of every quilt shop. It was available in clear, translucent, opaque, and colored varieties.

Unlikely Sources of Tools

Freezer paper was also pressed into service as an aid to accurate piecing. The matte side of the paper was good for tracing templates for the most complex or original pieced patterns. The shiny, waxy side would temporarily adhere to fabrics when pressed with a warm iron. To cut patches, quilters simply eyeballed a seam allowance width beyond the edge of the freezer paper. Hand-piecers especially loved matching the corners and edges of fabric patches, and using freezer paper made this challenging assembly doable and accurate.

Another essential, the zipper-topped baggie, helped quilters keep track of myriad pieces and made hand piecing a portable project. Quilters adopted Post-it® notes and other sticky-backed papers from the office supply store to keep everything labeled and organized. Discovered in the art store, silver, white, or yellow pencils were drafted to mark around templates on dark fabrics, while vellum was useful for paper-foundation piecing.

"It's true I use some pretty high-tech tools, such as a computer drawing program, for designing, but what do I love most? Freezer paper. It has simplified my life. I trace a full-sized cartoon for my design onto freezer paper, and I use it to stabilize each piece, so that everything fits together very precisely."

-Caryl Bryer Fallert

The Biggest Thing Since Sliced Bread

In the early 1970s, new handles on dressmakers shears and embroidery scissors made cutting layers of fabric and trimming "dog ears" much more comfortable to do. Imported from Europe, Fiskars® and Gingher® scissors quickly cut themselves a prominent place in the sewing and quilting supplies market. But ask any quilter what the biggest change, not just in cutting tools but in quiltmaking in general, was during the last thirty years of the twentieth century, and chances are excellent she'll point to the rotary cutter. Even devotees of appliqué who only piece to join Baltimore Album blocks will agree. This little tool, with its round, rolling, razor-sharp blade, endowed quilters with both accuracy and speed. With the rotary cutter and

Olfa's original rotary cutter.
Photo courtesy of Brian Sheldon/Olfa North American.

a few accessories, quilters could create ten times the number of pieced quilt tops their mothers or grandmothers could in the same amount of time, with equally precise results.

The rotary revolution had a domino effect. Nancy Srebro-Johnson explains the financial effects: "So now quiltmakers will buy ten times more fabric, ten times more thread, ten times more batting. One builds upon the other." Because of the rotary cutter, there was a major shift in attitude and focus for manufacturers and home sewers. Before the rotary cutter came onto the scene, the sewing machine, fabric, and notions industries were totally geared to making dresses and curtains. After rotary cutting established itself, the market for quiltmaking caught up with and surpassed all other sewing and needle-art segments of the market.

Once Around the Rotary

The rotary cutter was developed in the 1970s at a company in Japan called Olfa, to cut multiple layers of silk fabrics for kimono production. In 1979, Barbara Sweetman, then the owner of Yarn Loft International (YLI) in California, was given a rotary cutter by her father, who had noticed it during one of his many business trips to Japan. Barbara, in turn, brought the tool to Marti Michell. Marti recalls, "There was no mat, no ruler, and I said to her, 'We can't use that, it will ruin the tabletop.'"

Coincidentally, Marti had recently hired Mary Ellen Hopkins, an innovative quilt teacher, to teach classes for her company. Mary Ellen had been using narrow transparent acrylic strips to mark straight lines on fabric before scissor cutting, and she happened to try rotary cutting along the edge of one of the acrylic strips. "To me, that was the beginning," says Marti, commenting on the key combination of rotary cutter and rotary ruler. Cutting mats to protect tabletops quickly completed the essential trinity.

On a *Simply Quilts* television program that first aired in 1997, host Alex Anderson reflected, "Scissors became a dinosaur, didn't they?" Her guest on that show, Mary Ellen Hopkins, quickly countered, "Well, I still have 'em for cutting thread."

Bob Ahrend, who handled the North American marketing and distribution for Olfa, remembers, "That first rotary cutter in 1979 had a blade 28 millimeters in diameter and came with refill blades. By 1981, we had a 45-millimeter blade." This size quickly became the most popular, because it could cut through more layers. Building on that astounding success, Olfa brought out the 60-millimeter cutter three years later. Beginning in the mid-1980s, Fiskars, Kai,

"I've got six 18"-by-24" cutting mats taped together to create a huge cutting surface. Just like other men with their vehicles, I've gotta have the biggest I can get."
–John Flynn

and Dritz® imported their own versions, each with its own special features, such as built-in storage for a spare blade, wavy-edged blades for special effects, and cutters with handles that are skinny, curved, or ergonomically correct.

Rotary Rulers and Templates

The earliest rulers made expressly for pairing with the rotary cutter were thick strips, without measurement guidelines. If you wanted to cut a 2" wide fabric strip, you had to use the 2" wide ruler. Nancy Crow brought a better idea to quilters. In the mid-1970s, Nancy's husband noticed how she labored over marking strips for her quilts, so he thoughtfully cut 3" wide clear Plexiglass strips left over from making storm door windows. He scribed each strip with a variety of lines for measuring. In 1984, a version of this inventive tool became the first universal rotary ruler that allowed for rotary cutting strips of various widths. EZ Quilting® marketed it as the Quickline® Ruler by Nancy Crow.

Also arriving on the scene were departures from rectangular rulers, including squares, triangles, and all manner of rotary templates for cutting specific shapes. The first triangle rulers developed for strip-piecing shaped angles were Kaye Wood's Starmaker® Master Templates in 1981, followed by a thick, acrylic version a couple of years after that. Other early specialty rulers in the mid-1980s were the Bias Square Ruler®, designed by Nancy J. Martin and Marsha McCloskey, and the Clearview Triangle by Sara Nephew. Shar Jorgenson's Double Wedding Ring templates also appeared on the scene. Most of these new templates, however, could be hard to find, and it took a while for the new rulers to gain recognition from the quilters.

Since the mid-1990s, rotary rulers and rotary templates, designed for cutting a specific shape, have been available in a "mind-boggling variety," as described by Dixie Haywood in a report for *Quilter's Newsletter Magazine*. To her amazement, she found few quilters who considered the large number overkill. From beginner to expert, quilters would buy any ruler that made it easier and faster to cut a specific shape. Square rulers, rulers for 45- and 60-degree angles, rulers for odd angles, wedges for fans and Dresden Plate patterns, hexagons for Grandmother's Flower Garden—all were scooped up. Simply by word-of-mouth promotion, the most versatile rulers achieved phenomenal success. Probably the best seller ever has been the Tri-Recs™, designed by Joy Hoffman and Darlene Zimmerman for Wrights®, with more than 10,000 units sold in the year 2000 alone. Tri-Recs combines, in one package, two templates for cutting various-sized trian-

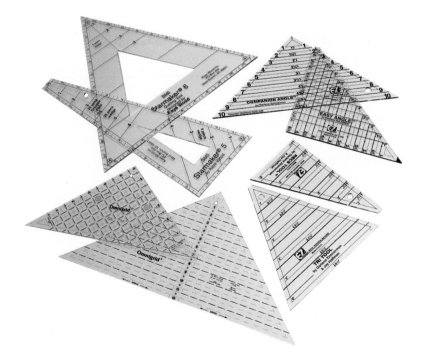

gles—one for an isosceles triangle (the Tri), the other for a bisected rectangle (the Recs). Together they help piecers create a Flying Geese block and many other designs.

Liberation!

The rotary-cutting revolution meant that quilters could fly through an entire border of Flying Geese, build Log Cabin blocks in next to no time, and rocket through a star-patterned quilt. The speed and ease of cutting freed quilters from endless, tedious projects. Not only that, but the liberation started by the rotary cutter spread to every phase of quiltmaking.

Strip Piecing

For the quilters of the 1980s and 1990s, the major appeal of rotary cutting was the ease in cutting long strips. With folded fabric and long rotary rulers, a quiltmaker could slice up lengths of fabric to accommodate any size of project. Those who preached safe rotary cutting also devised many new ways to rotary cut, piece sets of strips together, and cross-cut through a strip-set to produce pieced units, blocks, and borders—a process known as strip piecing.

Actually, strip piecing and other speed techniques had been around for a long time before the rotary cutter arrived. Marie Webster's 1915 book, *Quilts: Their Story and How to Make Them*, shows a Roman Stripe quilt done with strip-sets. At least as far back as the 1920s, the Amish used strip piecing to create Bars, Rail Fence, Streak o' Lightning, and many other patterns. Around that same time, the women of the Seminole tribe in Florida began offsetting ripped strips to adorn their clothing. About 1974, Ernest B. Haight of David City, Nebraska, came out with a small brochure that showed how to use two pieces of cloth to produce half-square triangles. Barbara Johannah (pronounced Yo-hawn'-ah) took that idea, plus those of Seminole patchwork, and wedded them to geometry. Her highly successful books, *Quick Quilting* in 1976 and *The Quick Quiltmaking Handbook* in 1979, revealed the template-free techniques she developed. Called "the woman who single-handedly changed the quilting world," Barbara ushered in time-saving, precision-oriented, assembly-line techniques.

Other quilters jumped on the fast-moving bandwagon. Cheryl Greider Bradkin showed the way to make more complex designs in *The Seminole Patchwork Book*, published in 1980. In 1981, Michael James threw light on his famously artful strip piecing in *The Second Quiltmaker's Handbook*. In her 1982 workbook, *The It's Okay If You Sit on My Quilt Book*, Mary Ellen Hopkins showed how to create 350 patchwork patterns and designs by using only squares, right triangles, and strips.

In the late 1970s, Eleanor Burns was inspired by the refuse of a garment manufacturer. As her Web site explains, her find was "a long string of trouser

"Before 1990, the mentality would be, if I can make two quilts a year, that's my goal. From 1994 on, quiltmaking progressed by leaps and bounds because the monkey was off people's backs. The 'quilt police' were no longer hovering to say you had to cut with scissors, piece or quilt by hand, or even do the quilting at all."

-Nancy Srebro-Johnson

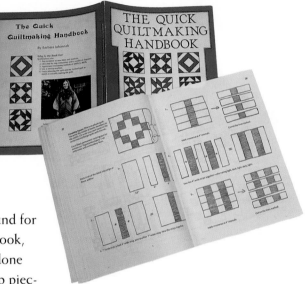

Barbara Johannah's how-to books introduced strip piecing to the quilt world.

"Barbara Johannah did for quiltmaking what the Cuisinart food processor did for cooking—she showed us there's a faster way!"
-Mary Mashuta

"For my boys whose vans never seem to have a working heater, for my daughter who is currently supporting the nail polish industry while sitting cross-legged on the bed with her friends, and for my friends who drink cocoa in bed—yes, it's OK if you sit on my bed. Why? Because I've learned secrets about cutting and piecing that make it possible for me to make quilts in a fraction of the time you would expect without sacrificing design."
-Mary Ellen Hopkins

waistbands, joined in a continuous strip, with pockets attached every couple of feet." The light bulb came on, and a variety of speed-piecing techniques were the result. She was already used to ripping strips and finding ways to make difficult things simple. Fondly called the First Lady or the Queen Bee of Quilting, Eleanor brought her clever ideas to other quilters through her *Quilt in a Day* TV shows and workshops.

Speed Piecing Grows the Market

Along with speed piecing came a lot of other speedy new notions. Quilters discovered that they could place a rotary ruler right over flat, flower-headed pins (imported from Japan in 1992 by Collins), pull them out in a flash, and fling them over to a magnetic pincushion. Also new were small and revolving cutting mats for cutting small pieces, and mini-irons and small ironing surfaces for quick pressing. Improved features made thread clippers, seam rippers, and stilettos precious to the quick quiltmaker. The speed-piecing craze also increased the sales of dozens if not hundreds of how-to books filled with pieced-quilt designs. Titles featured words like "quick," "fast," "speedy," or "time-saving."

Sewing Machines

Many a quilter started out in the 1970s with her mother's or grandmother's Singer® sewing machine. Singer popularized an installment payment plan that made sewing machines affordable, and therefore omnipresent, in mid-twentieth century homes. Sears competed for customers with their popularly priced Kenmore models, and later Brother® machines entered the fray. As quilters' skill levels improved, they were drawn to imported machines, with industrial strength and versatility, made by companies such as Bernina®, Elna, Husqvarna Viking, Janome/New Home, and Pfaff®. Fully electronic machines made their debut in 1986. And as quilting rose in popularity, all machine manufacturers began enticing prospective quilters with new and special features. Foremost among them was the patchwork foot.

Notions for speed piecing.

The Perfect ¼"

Quilters quickly learned that beautiful patchwork quilts required accurate stitching, in addition to accurate cutting and pressing. Consistent ¼" seam allowances were the hallmark of excellence, and a ¼" or patchwork presser foot on a sewing machine was the ticket to success. The Little Foot®, introduced by Lynn Graves in 1989, was the first such accessory. It fit onto most machines, though sometimes a separate adapter was necessary. Elna,

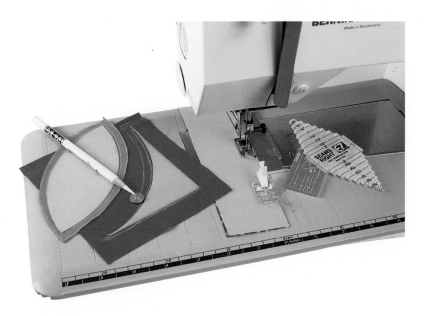

Handy helps for ¼" seams.

Janome/New Home, Bernina, Viking, and Pfaff all followed suit with their own patchwork presser feet. Models by Little Foot, Viking, and Pfaff featured marked lines to aid in stopping, starting, and pivoting. Bernina's foot had an indentation that allowed sewers to gauge a ⅛" seam allowance, which was helpful for making miniature quilts. Some machines also permitted the piecer to shift the needle position, in very slight increments, to one side or the other of the center, for fine tuning seam allowance width. Without these features on her sewing machine, a quilter could still achieve a perfect ¼" seam allowance by searching quilt shops and catalogs for generic metal or plastic seam guides. If she preferred, she could cut up moleskin strips to adhere to the throat plate at the proper distance from the needle, creating a splendid guide.

Quilters prized other new sewing-machine features: 1986 saw the first fully electronic machine, and with the '90s came the needle up/down button and the knee lever. Setting the needle to always stop down in the fabric guaranteed smooth seam lines and smooth machine-quilting lines as well. The knee lever lifted the presser foot for stops and restarts, leaving hands free to guide the work as the piecer sped through a chain of paired patches like a NASCAR racer on a mission. This feature was also handy for machine appliquérs, easing the navigation of curves and points.

The Seam Not Seen

In the 1980s, thread makers began to cater to quilters' needs. Nancy Srebro-Johnson remembers, "Back in the beginning, before the proliferation of quilt shops, we bought the only kind of thread available in the chain stores—polyester-coated thread. The mentality of quiltmaking was, 'It's gotta last for life, and polyester thread was gonna hold this puppy together forever!' But people realized that the polyester thread was cutting the fabric over time and wasn't healthy for our quilts." Quilters learned to match the fiber content of their threads to their 100 percent cotton fabrics, and to expect, and get, longevity with a fifty-weight cotton thread that featured a smooth, silky finish.

Block Party

Even before the introduction of rotary cutting, patchwork blocks commanded most of the attention in quiltmaking. In the 1970s, most quilters built their quilt designs with traditional patchwork blocks. These easy, classic squares were the basic building blocks for scrap quilts and charm quilts, and a direct path to the oh-so-popular country look. Doing patchwork was considered a rendezvous with history and a way of producing quilts that guests might look upon as antique heirlooms. Blocks were the blockbuster hit of the quilt world.

The 1980's brought news on the block. Judy Martin, a *Quilter's Newsletter Magazine* editor and the author of many books, was best known for starting with a traditional block and putting a new spin on it. A prodigious number of her new and popular block designs appeared throughout the 1980s and 1990s. Judy also influenced many conventions in pattern presentation, precision piecing with templates, and effective settings for blocks.

Beloved Basics

Throughout America's history, the Log Cabin has been the most popular quilt pattern. Everyone recognized the pattern, named in a nostalgic nod to the old homestead. Quilters found it the easiest block of all to construct, especially utilizing those easy-to-cut strips. Between 1970 and 2000, quilters erected thousands of traditional Log Cabin masterpieces. And new and different architectural variations on this pattern rivaled the diversity of plans for real log homes. Quilt designers placed the "chimney square" off-center, made the logs surrounding it different widths, or skewed the block. With so many inspiring examples, quiltmakers of all skill levels found innovation as easy as, well, falling off a log.

Judy Martin's *Ultimate Book of Quilt Block Patterns,* 1988, gave patterns for these original blocks and many more.
Photo by Birlauf & Steen Photography.

SQUARE WITHIN A SQUARE, WITHIN A SQUARE
(102" x 102", 1986). A traditional tour de force
by Ruth B. Smalley.
Permanent collection of the
Museum of the American Quilter's Society.

LOG CABIN AND STARS
(50" × 60", 1997). Gwen Marston liberated
the Log Cabin block with unplanned,
random logs.

UJOH (WARMTH OF HEART)
(57" × 75½", 1989) was one of
Emiko Toda Loeb's early reversible
Log Cabin art quilts.
Photo by Mickey Faeder.

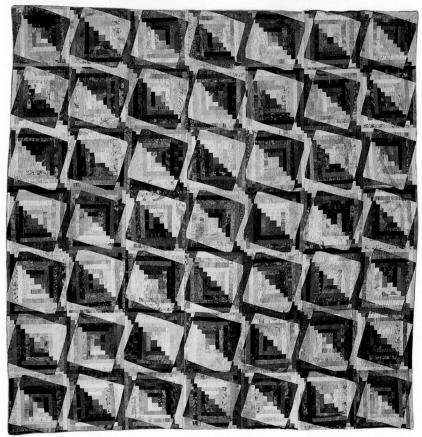

DANCING LOG CABIN
(80" × 80", 2000).
Katie Pasquini Masopust
made diagonal cuts in her
blocks to make them dance.

Kaleidoscopic Options

Another block that appealed to traditionalists and innovators alike was the Kaleidoscope. This pie-slice piecing, with many points coming together at the center, demanded more patience and attention than the Log Cabin. To keep it quick and easy, Sally Schneider used her assembly-line techniques, and Sharon Newman and Bobbie Aug linked paper piecing and string quilting. Because of its intricacy, the Kaleidoscope was a favorite showcase for the slow-and-steady quilter who had no truck for speed and ease, the type who took pride in meticulous accuracy. Katie Pasquini Masopust's mandalas and Jinny Beyer's Kaleidoscopes were much admired as wonders of complexity. Although these works were made doable through the use of clear plastic templates and elaborate border prints, hand piecing and touches of hand appliqué intimidated anyone seeking a weekend project. Taking this genre to the max was Paula Nadelstern. Her stunningly intricate piecing mimicked the glass-and-mirrors effect produced by the most complicated kaleidoscopes.

In 1998, Bethany Reynolds shared her strategy for conquering the Kaleidoscope. Her Stack-n-Whack® method of carefully layering a single print fabric to align the pattern repeats allowed quilters to easily rotary-cut a number of identical wedges at one time. The technique caught on faster than you can say, "Bethany's books were bestsellers."

SUMMER BOUQUETS
(56" x 63", 1997). A Stack-n-Whack®
Kaleidoscope by Bethany S. Reynolds.

KALEIDOSCOPIC XV: ECCENTRIC CIRCLES
(59" x 75½", 1995) by Paula Nadelstern.
Photo by Karen Bell.

REFLECTIONS (37½" × 34", 1994)
by Frances B. Calhoun.
Photo by John P. Hamel.
Photo courtesy of Rodale, Inc.

Bowing to the Past

Many other traditional designs were revisited, revitalized, and revamped with innovative fabrics and techniques that offered more speed and greater precision. Many accomplished quilters and artists made a name for themselves based on their devotion to a particular pieced classic. Judy Mathieson pointed the way to drafting and piecing Mariner's Compass, a complex star used in American quilts since as early as 1830. John Flynn had a serious fling with Double Wedding Ring, and Susan L. Stein seemed to marry herself to it. Dixie Haywood was dubbed the queen of crazy quilts, updating the genre with random piecing over batting, and Marsha McCloskey soared with Feathered Stars (see STAR OF CHAMBLIE on page 49).

Taking advantage of the huge palette of fabrics in the 1990s, quilters seized upon a simple One-Patch mosaic of squares and waded into watercolor quilts. Meanwhile, the classic Bars designs got stretched and strip-pieced to produce Bargello quilts. Strip piecing made both these patchwork genres easy.

CHRISTMAS WEDDING
(42" × 54", 1988) by John F. Flynn.
Photo by the artist.

JANE STICKLE QUILT.
In the collection of the
Bennington Museum, Bennington, Vermont.
The original 1863 inspiration by Jane Stickle.

Jane-iacs!

In 1863, Jane A. Stickle, at the peak of her technical and artistic abilities, created an amazing quilt composed of 169 blocks-some traditional, others original. Each block was a 4 1/2-inch-square marvel of advanced geometry. Including the equally intricate border, the quilt had a total of 5,602 pieces. Brenda Manges Papadakis saw the quilt in a book and fell in love with it. She showcased the quilt, part of the Bennington (Vermont) Museum collection, in her 1996 pattern book, *Dear Jane: The Two Hundred Twenty-five Patterns from the 1863 Jane A. Stickle Quilt.* Brenda introduced each section with "Dear Jane," as though writing to Jane Stickle herself. Almost instantly the Dear Jane movement swept quilters up in a near obsession with the "mother quilt." Since Brenda's book came out, Dear Jane fans have devoted themselves to recreating these pieced blocks, frequently using the new repro fabrics on the market.

Block Sets & Medallions

Quilters injected creativity into their quilts with their own unique arrangement of blocks, sashing, lattices, cornerstones, and borders. Quilt shops and magazines kept interest high with a "Block of the Month" feature, which, combined with blocks from other months, created an exciting Sampler quilt. Teachers showed how one strong repeated block could be powerful, but two alternating blocks could produce a sensational secondary pattern. Pioneers of quilt settings, such as Sharyn Craig and Margaret Miller, showed quiltmakers just how to turn different-sized or overly busy blocks into exciting, well-balanced compositions. Famous for her ebullient personality, Doreen Speckmann demonstrated how to play with imaginary friends "Peaky" (a half rectangle) and "Spike" (an isosceles triangle).

Medallion quilts, made with an important central design surrounded by a series of bordering sections, offered another way to piece together the elements. One shining example of such a quilt is Jinny Beyer's RAY OF LIGHT, the winner among more than 10,000 entries in the 1978 Great American Quilt Contest, and

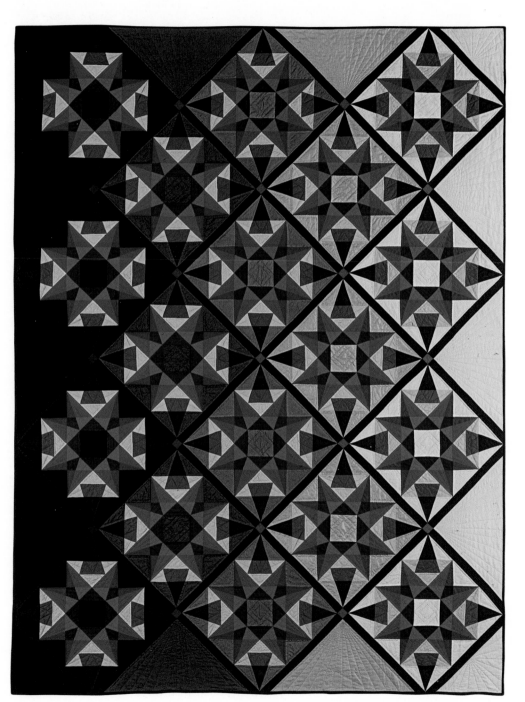

THE BLADE (62" x 84", 1985)
by Doreen Speckmann.
In the collection of the Museum of the American Quilter's Socitey.

RAY OF LIGHT (80" x 91", 1977) by Jinny Beyer.

later chosen as one of the Twentieth Century's 100 Best American Quilts. It features a Mariner's Compass design in the center, surrounded by a mosaic of blocks set on point. Jinny lived in India for years and incorporated fabrics from the Far East in her quilt. The medallion arrangement calls to mind a prayer rug. Jinny warmly notes that her daughter, born in India, is named Kiran—a Hindi word meaning ray of light. Jinny's second book, *The Art and Technique of Creating Medallion Quilts*, came out in 1982.

Caution: Sharp Curves Ahead

Joining edges that were not straight struck fear in the hearts of the most experienced devotees of patchwork quilting. Those who wended their way into curved piecing were often those who had honed their sewing skills making clothing. As designer Elaine Plogman says, "I began using curves and circles in quilts before I suspected there was anything to fear. I had been setting sleeves into dresses since high school and found curved-seam piecing in quilts was easier because at least the grain lines of the concave and convex pieces were similar." She sang the praises of sewing machine advances for better control for tight curves: the knee lift, the needle down, and the free arm. Helping to demystify curves was Joyce Schlotzhauer, who developed the curved two-patch system.

Judy B. Dales offered dreamscapes of graceful commas and swirls in her quilts. Sharing her secrets, she lived up to her name, teaching quilters to match the hills and dales of curvy fabric edges and sew on the dale side. Virginia Walton used templates for piecing curves without pins, for classic designs like Drunkard's Path.

Foundation Piecing

Anyone who could stitch on a line learned she could do foundation piecing. Though the technique of sewing to a foundation of paper or muslin was popular in the nineteenth century, several advances in the 1980s and 1990s revitalized the technique. In the early 1980s, companies, such as Graphic Impressions, offered rubber stamps for inking designs onto muslin. Light boxes aided in tracing designs from a pattern. Dixie Haywood and Jane Hall adapted foundation techniques to paper. They popularized two different techniques: "top-pressed piecing" in which the pattern lines are fabric placement lines and the stitching is done with the fabric on top, and "under-pressed piecing" in which the pattern lines are sewing lines and the seams are sewn with the paper foundation on top. This second technique won enormous and lasting favor with quiltmakers.

Like Dixie and Jane, Carol Doak loved the accuracy of piecing to a foundation and preferred a removable paper foundation, leaving her with fewer layers to penetrate for hand quilting. Carol used the design-drawing feature of *Electric Quilt*™ software to create sixty-five quilt block designs for her 1994 book *Easy Machine Paper Piecing*. This book attracted quilters of all skill levels back to the time-honored piecing method.

Paper piecing was very popular in the 1990s.

FANTASY FORM #1634 (57" x 40", 1995)
by Judy B. Dales.
Photo by Karen Bell.

From the mid-1990s on, packets of printed foundation papers were a hot commodity with quilters. Even those who couldn't draw a picture or draft a simple block could piece a complex block pattern with a plethora of animals, flowers, and other homey objects. By the end of the 1990s, Benartex carried preprinted "Foundation by the Yard," designed by Sharon Hultgren; Handler was selling a marked interfacing; and Graphic Impressions, which had once sold rubber stamps, was distributing a stabilizer called Easy Tear, which could be torn away or left in place. With translucent vellum, quilters could trace, photocopy, or scan designs from their home computers.

At the same time, artists adopted foundation piecing for perfect renditions of classic designs: Karen Stone for Empire Beauty and Indian Orange Peel; Caryl Bryer Fallert for Flying Geese; and Barbara Olson for spirals of spikey sawteeth. Quilts incorporating foundation piecing received many major awards, drawing even more attention to this innovative piecing technique.

IN THE BEGINNING (59" x 59", 1994). Barbara Olson uses foundation piecing to achieve precision. From the collection of Quilts, Inc. Photo by Jim Lincoln, courtesy of Quilts, Inc.

Minis Take Piecing to the Max

Refined piecing techniques inspired results that had never been seen before and sparked rising excitement among quilters. Looking at a large intricately pieced quilt, viewers were wowed by the number of pieces precisely fit. And at every show where miniature quilts were included, the reaction turned to awe. "How did she ever do that?" was part of every conversation. In this category, Sally Collins enjoyed a prestigious reputation for her attainment of small-scale perfection. Tina Gravatt miniaturized more than two hundred quilt classics, some of which she displayed on vintage doll beds. George Siciliano, new to quilting after admiring his wife's splendid quilts, set himself the task of including thousands of patches in his foundation-pieced Pineapple variations, each quilt less than a square foot in size. Mini-quilt makers discovered that working on a small scale could be just as time-consuming as making a full-sized bed covering.

Big or small, traditional or innovative, speedy or slow, scrappy or planned, there was something to appeal to every patchwork enthusiast. As the number of piecers and quilts grew exponentially, so did the public perception of people who cut up fabric only to stitch it together again. As a result, today we hear, "Quilters should have their heads examined!" a lot less often. Much more common come the raves, "Look at these patchwork masterpieces!"

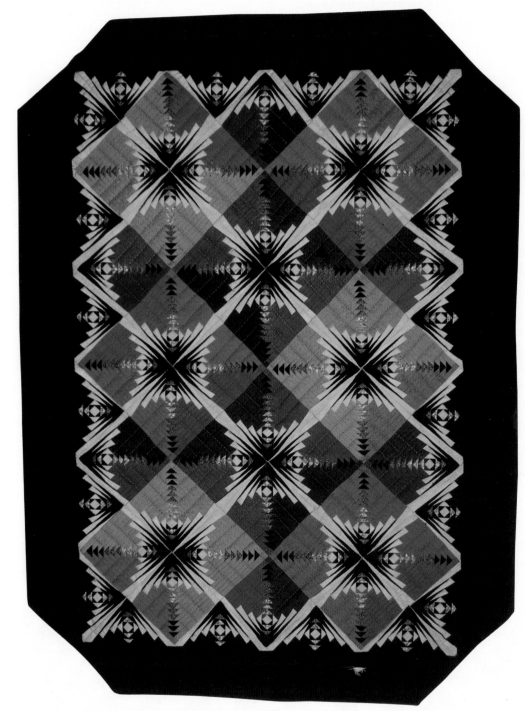

CROP CIRCLES
(15½" x 21", 1999) by George Siciliano.
Photo by the artist.

Appliquéing Our Quilts: Refinement & Revolution

The term "appliqué" (the technique by which pieces are applied onto a background) summons a strong, emotional response from just about every quiltmaker. "From the very beginning," says Sue Nickels, "I've loved appliqué. I think you can be more artistic, and just like the Baltimore Album makers of old, you can portray images with real symbolism, tell a story, leave a legacy."

Some people who appliqué prefer to use another term. When Jinny Beyer incorporates it into her quiltmaking, she calls it "soft-edge piecing." Caryl Bryer Fallert falls back on it when the need arises, but refers to her technique as "appli-piecing." And the word, with all its traditional connotations, is something Melody Johnson, Laura Wasilowski, and Robbie Joy Eklow politely avoid if not downright refuse to use. "Fusing" is how they speak of their niche.

SPRING WINDS (76" x 87", 1987)
by Faye Anderson.
In the collection of the
Museum of the American Quilter's Society.

"There's a wonderful freedom in appliqué. Flowers and leaves can sway in the wind, and fish can swim backward in the water if I want them to. Best of all, I don't have to worry about cutting off patchwork points! Appliqué designs do not have to fit precisely together like puzzle pieces."
                                                    -Mimi Dietrich
                    -from Basic Quiltmaking Techniques for Hand Appliqué.

Mission Impossible

During the period between 1970 and 2000, those Americans interested in quiltmaking considered the legacy of appliqué from great-grandmother's generation admirable, but such "fancy-work," as it was called, was downright intimidating. Who had that much time to put into creating a family quilt? The '30s and '40s had brought many appliquéd patterns and kits that were a lot simpler and less time consuming, but the appeal of butterflies, Sunbonnet Sues, and state flowers in soft pastels was, for the most part, lost on women in the '70s.

For anyone tempted to learn traditional appliqué techniques, reading the written instructions in magazines of the '70s and '80s was enough to dampen enthusiasm, and following those directions was liable to squelch one's interest altogether. Simply preparing each appliqué pattern was an enormous chore. First of all, patterns usually appeared reduced on a grid. In the days before there were photocopiers with enlargement functions on every block in town (let alone in most homes), it was necessary to draw a grid the size of the appliqué motif desired and transfer the pattern lines, box by box, to the new grid. Often, the portion thus transferred was only a half or a quarter of the pattern. Next, the traced pattern had to be glued to a cardboard backing which was stiff enough to trace around. It's no wonder editors chose to include fewer appliqué than pieced quilts in any quilt magazine's pattern offerings. It was common knowledge that readers liked looking at them, but few would actually make them.

Early Self-Help Alternatives

Jean Ray Laury's first book, *Appliqué Stitchery*, published in 1966, was one of the few appliqué guides on the market during the 1970s. Her designs appeared in many mainstream women's magazines, attracting notice to her unique brand of appliqué. It was only later that Jean realized just how unique it was—"After *Quilts and Coverlets* came out (1970), I was appalled that I'd had the nerve to write a book on a subject I knew so little about! But perhaps that was okay, because it put me in the same position as anyone who might read the book."

Whether she was tucking edges under or using cutouts of felt that wouldn't unravel, Jean Ray Laury used tiny running stitches, often in a contrasting color, to adhere each piece. "I was told repeatedly, early on, 'That's not the way to appliqué. You have to hide the stitches.' My work was often sniffed at because the stitches showed." But Jean defended her self-taught style. "The evidence of hand stitching adds an element to any work that is very important. The involvement of the hand, the craftsmanship, is vital. I like seeing the means of attachment become a strong element of the design." Many people agreed with this philosophy, but throughout the last twenty years, the furor over visible appliqué stitches repeatedly peaked and ebbed.

Jean's stitches were not her only innovation. The folk-art whimsy of her motifs was fresh and influential. Her posies were simple and bold, and she often included mushrooms and fruits, both whole and sliced open. A child's quilt was likely to feature the receiver's personal favorites in toys, desserts, and pastimes.

"Piecework was the focus of the early 1970s quilt revival.... Appliqué seemed both difficult and dull to women who itched to stitch every possible variation of the Log Cabin and Drunkard's Path."

-Barbara Brackman

TOM'S QUILT (74" x 30", 1956) by Jean Ray Laury.
This quilt appeared in her 1970 book, *Quilts and Coverlets.*
Photo by Stan Bitters-Sculptor.

Purple Passion Coat (1972),
by Virginia Avery.

Back View: Purple Passion Coat (1972),
by Virginia Avery.

In 1978, another guide, *The Big Book of Appliqué* by Virginia Avery, presented a bounty of designs. The book spotlighted specific designers and called attention to their personal vocabularies for appliqué, suggesting innovative solutions and alternatives to tradition. Virginia's own appliqué work, especially on her garments, demonstrated her distinctive flair and irreverent spirit.

An Appliqué Master

Chris Wolf Edmonds was one of the talents spotlighted in *The Big Book of Appliqué*. Like Jean Ray Laury, Chris chose appliqué imagery that was far from traditional, but totally in tune with the times. Moreover, her technique and needle skills were impeccable. Chris first came to the attention of an admiring quilt world when her portrait quilt, GEORGE WASHINGTON AT VALLEY FORGE, won first prize at the National Bicentennial Quilt Exhibit and Contest in Warren, Michigan, in 1976. Unusual for the time, a large single image dominates the piece, owing to Chris's use of an opaque projector. While Chris had no formal art training, her work showed the quilt world that appliqué could convey pictures with touching realism. Moreover, her kits in the early 1980s attracted newcomers to appliqué. Her fan base was relieved they didn't have to commit to a huge, daunting project to try appliqué. Nor did they have to deal

GEORGE WASHINGTON AT VALLEY
FORGE (78" × 92", 1976)
by Chris Wolf Edmonds.
Photo by John Bradbury.

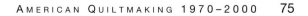

with troublesome bindings and other finishing details. These folksy, seasonal motifs or scenes were designed to be quilted and displayed in hoops. They were often used to decorate doors, hence the nickname "welcome quilts."

Grace and Charm

One can easily argue that Baltimore Album style is the most successful revival within quilting. Since the beauty of Baltimore Album quilts came to public attention in museum collections, many who would never have ventured into fancy work were smitten. Foremost among them was Elly Sienkiewicz, who lived close enough to Baltimore and to the National Library of Congress in Washington, D.C., to make it possible for her to study Baltimore quilts and patterns. "Seeing Baltimore Album quilts changed my life," says Elly. "I felt as if I were looking into the souls of the women who made them." Because of her 1983 book, *Spoken Without a Word*, sixteen subsequent books, and many popular workshops, Elly got much of the credit for relaunching Baltimore Album style. In doing so, she ushered in a host of other needle-arts revivals: cutwork, embroidery (including silk-ribbon embroidery), ribbonwork, ruching, yo-yos, calligraphy, and inked drawings. Making Baltimore Album quilts is, for Elly, "holding hands with the past while pointing to the future."

Beyond Baltimore

Inspired by this gracious, traditional appliqué style, other artists "came to Baltimore," bringing their own individual flair for design. Jeana Kimball, who made one of the blocks in GOOD LADIES OF BALTIMORE, authored *Reflections of Baltimore*, which came out in 1981. Jeana soon began using her considerable needle-turn appliqué skills to express Baltimore Album in a countrified style, enlivened by leaping hares and birds on the wing.

GOOD LADIES OF BALTIMORE (detail)

GOOD LADIES OF BALTIMORE
(91" x 91", 1988). A group quilt designed, led, and blocks made in part by Elly Sienkiewicz. Border appliquéd by Agnes Cook; quilting by Virgina Lemasters and Carol Jo White.
Photo by Melissa Karlin Mahoney.
Courtesy of *Quilter's Newsletter Magazine*.

FAIRMEADOW (40" x 40", 1992)
by Jeana Kimball.

Backgrounds Come to the Fore

Until the mid-1980s, the vast majority of appliquéd quilts, and Baltimore Albums in particular, were fashioned on white or ecru backgrounds. Even the use of another pale solid was thought a daring decision. Even after a large variety of prints arrived in the marketplace, it took persistence and luck to find the quiet print that would provide a pretty setting but not upstage the starring role of the appliqué. Faye Anderson showed quilters the way. She chose soft gray and white floral prints as background fabrics for SPRING WINDS (see page 71), which won the American Quilter's Society Best of Show award in 1985. This was a turning point in Faye's work. "Since making this quilt, I have consciously tried to use prints rather than solids," she writes, "because it is pattern that most obviously distinguishes works in fabric from those in other mediums, such as paint."

Quiet visual texture soon made itself at home in the appliqué backgrounds of many quilts and became an important feature for any quiltmaker in search of a country look. Faye's work presaged the style of Becky Goldsmith and Linda Jenkins of Piece O' Cake Designs. Similarly, Faye's use of dark backgrounds was groundbreaking in the 1980s, and Patricia Campbell was one artist who used this contrast to great effect in her 1990s Jacobean masterpieces.

FLOURISHES (90⅛" × 90⅛", 1998) by Becky Goldsmith and Linda Jenkins of Piece O' Cake Designs. Photo by Marona Photography

JACOBEAN ARBOR
(80" × 80", 1989)
by Patricia B. Campbell.
Hand quilting by Jackie Muehlstein.

Revised Tradition

Other appliqué quilts that attracted attention and admiration in the 1980s are those by Nancy Pearson, Laura Reinstatler, and Irma Gale Hatcher. Hanging in major quilt shows and appearing in popular books and magazines, these quilts are a combination of antique inspiration and original spirit, and they have wielded a strong influence on the "next generation" of appliqué enthusiasts.

Some artists, while adhering to tradition with their hand-appliqué techniques, proceeded to venture far afield for their subject matter. The song "The Twelve Days of Christmas" inspired a magnificent appliqué picture made by B.J. Elvgren in 1983. The architectural shape of the huge quilt gives a viewer the impression of peering into a fairy-tale theatre, with velvets, silk, trapunto, and embroidery adding to the richness. Velda Newman magnified flowers to glorious proportions, like a Georgia O'Keefe of the cloth. She dyed her own fabrics to get the exact shades she needed.

THE TWELVE DAYS OF CHRISTMAS (102" x 108", 1983) by B. J. Elvgren. In the collection of the Museum of the American Quilter's Society.

HYDRANGEA (detail).

HYDRANGEA (99" x 84", 1989)
by Velda E. Newman.

A soft spot for fauna, as well as flora, characterized many award-winning quilts by Suzanne Marshall and Charlotte Warr Andersen. Each of these artists was a master of hand appliqué, and their work won many awards and admiration in the 1980s and 1990s. Though their styles were completely different, both used unusual sources for their subject matter. Suzanne Marshall abandoned scrap-quilt piecing for appliqué in the early 1980s but continued to favor pieced-block constructions. After mastering Baltimore-Album style, Suzanne began scouting out classic source material, like architectural details, mosaic floor patterns, and fifteenth-century manuscript illustrations, as inspiration for her quilts. Squirrels and birds, beetles and bugs—either in silhouette or multi-layered—enliven many of her sampler and medallion quilts (see her quilt on page 30).

In the mid-1990s, Charlotte Warr Andersen literally gave a face to realistic human and pet portraiture. She used photos projected on the wall for results that seemed larger than life. Charlotte devised an interesting way of composing the elements, then auditioned various fabric choices for the background. "The faces for my quilts are constructed separately, and so is the background, using a reverse layering technique, sort of like doing a mola," she explains.

"I much prefer hand techniques. They just look nicer. I have a distinct prejudice against raw edges, and so I do needle-turn appliqué."
-Charlotte Warr Andersen

TELEPATHY (24"x 24", 1998)
by Charlotte Warr Andersen.
Photo by artist.

TELEPATHY (detail).

SHADOW BALTIMORE BRIDE
(90" x 108", 1987) by Marian H. Shenk.
In the collection of the
Museum of the American Quilter's Society.

Inspirations from Around the World

Borrowing from the needle arts and cultures of other times and places, many genres within the appliqué category arose in this revival.

Shadow appliqué.

To achieve a softly romantic look, shapes of bright-colored fabric are encased under a layer of bridal-veil tulle or other sheer fabric. The overlay gives them a soft, shadowy look. Quilting around the shapes holds them in place. While some quilters say this isn't really appliqué, it so closely mimics the look of appliqué that many have accepted it.

Stained glass.

Colorful shapes are cut out and basted in place. Their raw edges are covered with dark bias strips that simulate the leading in cathedral windows. Since Roberta Horton presented the stained glass technique in an adult education class in 1977, this genre has made converts of anyone looking for a change of pace. Single-fold bias tape removes the tedious step of preparing the "leading."

STAINED GLASS WINDOWS
(98" x 112", 1986) by Nadene Zowada.
In the collection of the
Museum of the American Quilter's Society.

Example of Hmong design.

Celtic appliqué.

Like stained glass, this appliqué form calls for prepared bias strips or commercial bias tape to recreate ancient motifs of the Emerald Isles. The strips are carefully intertwined over a background, then appliquéd in place.

Reverse appliqué.

In this technique, slits or cuts are made in an appliqué piece and the edges are turned back and blind-stitched to expose a layer underneath. This layer may be the background, as with cutwork, or it may be one or many progressive contrasting fabric inserts, as in molas from Central America. Quilt historian Judy Roche credits the Hmong (the H is silent) people among those who nurtured this art form. "The Hmong came here after the Vietnam War, and they brought their intricate unquilted appliqué rendered in panels and pillow covers. In attendance at every major quilt show and conference, Hmong family businesses helped make reverse appliqué mainstream."

Channel appliqué.

This is just another form of reverse appliqué, with slits in the top layer revealing the under layer for linear designs. Roxanne McElroy used this technique to recreate classic Calvin & Hobbs cartoons and other humorous slices of life. Meanwhile, Charlotte Patera updated the mola with designs reminiscent of cave drawings and petroglyphs.

CANYON COMMUNICATIONS
(54" x 37", 1996) by Charlotte Patera.
Photo by Steve Buckley,
Photographic Reflections.

GLIMPSES OF GLYPHS
(39" x 41", 1997) by Charlotte Patera.
Photo by Steve Buckley,
Photographic Reflections.

LINDA'S LACE
(60½" × 76", 1997)
by Linda Pool.
Photo by artist.

Detail showing cutwork applique.

Cutwork.

Linda Pool promoted this Victorian form of needlework with her award-winning LINDA'S LACE. Encouraging others to try this technique, the quiltmaker says, "It is a freer form of appliqué, as a 'mistake' can be easily fixed or adjusted so it is not even noticeable. The project need not be perfect in order to be truly beautiful, and this takes off the pressure to get everything just so." Scherenschnitte, a German folk art of paper cutting, also inspired cutwork appliqué designs.

Hawaiian appliqué.

No one really knows the exact origins of this distinctive hybrid quilt form. It seems to be a clever combination of two traditions: the woodblock-type patterning of bark cloth, made by Hawaiian women for generations, and the quilting skills—possibly Baltimore Album-style cutwork—brought and taught to these women by the wives of American missionaries, beginning in the early 1800s. Traditionally, Hawaiian appliqué starts with a large piece of fabric folded into eighths and cut, like the paper snowflakes everyone makes in grade school. Contemporary designers, such as Elizabeth Akana, use the same solid-color contrasts, tropical foliage imagery, and luxuriant echo quilting of their ancestors. Similarly, Roxanne McElroy shared the cultural and quilt traditions of her native Tahitian appliqué with designs folded into fourths. Her daughter Dierdre (Didi) continues to teach this traditional art.

ULU MAU ALOHA/
LOVE UNCONDITIONAL
(62" x 62", 1991) by Elizabeth Akana.
Photo by Sharon Risedorph.

A Frenzy of Fabulous New Products

After the spartan marketplace of the 1970s, the introduction of hundreds of new products made appliqué much more approachable and appealing to quiltmakers. Kits and pattern books abounded and presented actual-size appliqué patterns. In the late 1980s, big, sumptuous motifs in fabric designs suggested countless opportunities for single-unit appliqués that seemed to be made up of many pieces. Higher thread counts, or tighter weaves, meant seam allowances could be narrower without creating raveling disasters, which paved the way for the tiniest appliqué miniature quilts or itty-bitty details on larger masterworks.

By the mid-1990s, a wide variety of threads was available, delighting quilters everywhere. In 1999, Clover® began distributing Tire silk thread from Japan. With a fine, sleek surface, this thread embedded itself into the quilter's cottons almost invisibly, so there was no sign of hand stitching. Though costly, many quilters felt it was worth it. When machine appliqué first became popular, quilters discovered that the sixty-weight thread was a perfect choice. The Mettler® brand had been around since 1890 in just a few neutrals, but a hundred years later, the color choices had increased dramatically.

ULU MAU ALOHA/
LOVE UNCONDITIONAL, detail.

All manner of materials have cascaded out of the craft industry, particularly items that serve the needs of Baltimore Album devotees:

*Ribbons for embroidery and for folding, rolling, gathering, and ruching into three-dimensional flowers

*Embroidery threads and flosses perfect for stem-stitched tendrils

*Seed beads, bugle beads, and decorative threads to enhance the appliqué

*Silk flower petals, stamens, and leaves

*Tulle to encase tiny shapes and embellishments or tone down appliqués

Tools & Trends

Many appliqué tools were new during the '70s, '80s, or '90s, and a lot of them were crossover products from other hobby industries. Here's a brief rundown.

1979 Glue-sticks, which Collins adopted from the stationery store product, were found to be super for temporarily securing tiny appliqués in position.

1981 Clear, rigid, vinyl template sheets were introduced that were easy to position over a motif and cut with scissors.

1984 Extra-fine, extra-sharp silk pins were imported by Collins and Clover®.

1985 Silver pencils, discovered in an art supply store, left their mark on dark fabrics when quilters needed to trace around templates.

1986 Roxanne™ Quilter's Choice pencils came out in silver, which had been used to mark up X-rays, and in white.

1987 Nylon Bias Press Bars improved upon the metal press bars that had long been available for making bias stems and for doing stained glass and Celtic designs.

1989 Templar gave quilters a heat-resistant version of template plastic.

1990 (circa) Freezer paper was the new staple for appliqué, eliminating a lot of the marking, pinning, and tracing previously required.

1993 Straw, or milliner's needles, became the Cadillac for needle-turn appliqué.

1994 Appliqué sequin pins, a mere 1/2" to 3/4" long and considerably less likely than most pins to catch the thread, were imported.

1996 Roxanne™ Glue-Baste-It™ came out, with an orthodontist's syringe as an applicator tip.

1997 Bias tape maker, a gadget for making bias stems, was imported.

1999 Fusible bias tape on a roll was rolled out, in several colors.

1979 1981 1984 1985 1987 1989 1990 1993 1994 1996 1997 1999

The Fusible Phenomenon

Fusible web (a.k.a. fusible webbing, fusible adhesive, or just plain fusible) is a material that melts under the heat of an iron, forming an adhesive that promptly bonds fabrics together. Crafters were using fusible web in the '60s and '70s to decorate T-shirts, sweatshirts, pillows, and window shades. Everyone appreciated how it prevented cut edges from raveling. The first paper-backed fusible web, Wonder-Under® from Freudenberg NonWovens, came out in the mid-1960s. In 1986, a new and improved version was reintroduced. It was an immediate success with quilters because of what it didn't do: it didn't deteriorate within months, it didn't stiffen appliqués as much as its predecessors had; and it didn't gum up the sewing machine needle. Other companies soon brought out other brands of paper-backed fusible web, each with its own selling points.

"I know I owe my career to the inventor of this polyamide glue. I'd kiss him or her if I could find them. Fusing is fast and free and lets me express myself easily. Fortunately, fusing is becoming accepted in the art quilt world, and it's because of the beautiful pieces artists are making with the fusible web."
-Laura Wasilowski

IRONIC CONCLUSIONS
(45" x 53", 1996)
by Laura Wasilowski.
Photo by artist.

Since about 1993, Melody Johnson and Laura Wasilowski led the pack of quilt artists who used fusibles with wild abandon. While they always created their quilts separately, they were partners in selling their own hand-dyed fabrics. The two women pointed with pride to the excellent bond they got by fusing their own fabrics to a background, so that the tiniest pieces stayed put. They often incorporated a pinked or scalloped edge with their fusible-backed fabrics. As Melody explains, "I do not finish the edges of my shapes. The edges are often cut with a decorative rotary cutter blade, and I do not want to disturb that special edging."

At the end of the 1990s, Melody and Laura spent hour upon hour together in the car, driving from their Chicago-area homes to quilt shows around the country. There, they sold their hand-dyed fabrics and taught workshops on fusible appliqué and free-motion quilting. When these long, tiresome trips made them punchy or sleepy, they entertained themselves with jokes about their "Chicago School of Fusing," and made up "fight songs," which they set to popular tunes. Here's a sample:

> The minute you walked in the joint
> I could tell you were a presser of distinction
> A Real Big Fuser
> Sharp Scissors, an iron so fine
> O wouldn't you like to spend a little ROTARY time?
> So let me get right to the point
> I don't share my mat with folks who can't be free
> Hey Big Fuser!!
> Cut a little cloth with me!

Buttonhole appliqué became a popular genre in the '90s.

Sewing Machines Rev Up for Appliqué

A few years before fusibles became hot, technical advances in sewing machines led the way for the popularity of machine appliqué. Whereas sewing machines of the 1970s were strictly straight-stitchers, the new machines of the 1980s were generally zigzag machines, with a slot rather than a little hole in the throat plate, and an open-toed foot for the widest-swinging zigs and zags. With the machine set to a fine zigzag, and a thread with sheen, you could sew the most beautiful satin stitch, completely covering the raw edges of your appliqués. Some new machines gave you the blindstitch, not only great for hemming curtains, but a means of getting the look of hand-appliqué. In the 1990s, electronics provided dozens of decorative stitches that could be recruited for appliqué. Buttonhole stitch (the machine rendition of blanket stitch embroidery) quickly became the folk-art favorite. The quilter could now buy a machine that offered different speeds, and either take her time on small curves or put the pedal to the metal to machine-appliqué in long runs. Her new machine might also have a needle-down button, to ensure that machine zigzags and buttonhole stitches never skipped a beat when the work was paused or pivoted.

Machine Queens

Before the early 1990s, the majority of award-winning appliqué quilts featured traditional patterns and were hand-appliquéd. By the end of the decade, machine appliqué was in the lead. Two women in particular had a lot to do with that. Harriet Hargrave taught machine appliqué throughout the '80s. She developed many techniques to endow machine appliqué with an heirloom look. Beautifully rendered, these techniques were much admired for looking just like the "real thing," that is hand appliqué, and included various uses for freezer paper and blindstitching with clear nylon thread. These ideas and more

FLORAL URNS (90" x 90", 1993)
by Debra Wagner.
In the collection of the
Museum of the American Quilter's Society.

were compiled into her best-selling 1991 book, *Mastering Machine Appliqué*. Debra Wagner, who was Harriet's student, spread Harriet's gospel, but she also took the time to create several inspiring machine appliqué masterpieces. FLORAL URNS, in particular, won many awards, and it was designated one of the Twentieth Century's 100 Best American Quilts.

Sue Nickels admits to having learned many of her favorite techniques from Harriet and Debra. In fact, Sue's quilting career has been a veritable timeline of the trends in appliqué. Like most quilters, she spent quite a bit of time (1978-1987) exploring hand piecing and hand quilting. Her first foray into appliqué

ALBERTA ROSE
(85" × 85", 1993)
by Sue Nickels.

was in 1988. It was a hand-stitched flower and vine border added to the wide borders of a patchwork quilt. Many piecers similarly tiptoed into appliqué, seeking a way to fill an empty space or soften angular geometrics. Meanwhile, Sue was moving into machine piecing and machine quilting. The latter she quickly mastered and started teaching. It was only a short hop to machine appliqué.

In 1990, Sue tried and liked the "invisible" machine appliqué Harriet Hargrave taught and soon began using heat-resistant template plastic (see page 88) to turn the edges. She used these techniques on her ALBERTA ROSE, page 92, which could pass for a nineteenth-century masterpiece. Sue also experimented with visible machine-stitching effects, starting with straight stitches, in matching thread color, sewn along pressed appliqué edges. The next step was buttonhole or satin stitching done in a contrasting thread. It was a simple leap to the technique commonly called raw-edge appliqué, in which pieces are backed with fusible web (to prevent the edges from raveling), cut out along the sewing line, and pressed onto the background.

Sue recognized why most quiltmakers flocked to machine appliqué, "Originally, people came to machine techniques to save time, and the trade-off was that machine appliqué tended to look sloppy. But my sister, Pat Holly, and I would never compromise the quality of our work in the interest of speed. We use machine appliqué precisely because it gives the look we want."

From the late 1990s on, Sue saw a big improvement in quilters' appliqué skills and in their attitudes: "These days, machine appliqué is being accepted because it's done so well, and now we're at a point where I see novices going directly to the sewing machine as their primary tool, without the burden of learning the hand techniques first." Nevertheless, at the end of the millennium, machine appliqué still wasn't completely accepted or appreciated.

Sunbonnet Sue: Appliqué's Sweetheart

Sunbonnet Sue was the darling of Depression-era quilters and any appliqué stitcher with a hopeful—or hopeless—optimism. This chubby girl, whose face is forever hidden under her oversized sun hat, was born of the English illustrator Kate Greenaway. She was later adopted by Bertha Corbett, an American who, in 1902, illustrated The Sunbonnet Babies. Her countenance has graced thousands of quilts and provoked many a smile. However, some in the quilt world found her terminally cute (or perhaps a painful reminder of a "goody-two-shoes" past), and she became the subject of parody.

The most famous of these satirical quilts is undoubtedly THE SUN SETS ON SUNBONNET SUE, made in 1979. Twelve members of a sewing group, who dubbed themselves the "Seamsters' Union (Local #500)" of Lawrence, Kansas, appliquéd a total of twenty blocks, each depicting a different way to do away with Sue. One block shows Sue hanging from a noose; another has her collapsing in front of two nuclear reactor silos. She's struck by lightning, tied to railroad tracks, and swallowed by a gigantic boa constrictor, whose belly takes on Sue's familiar profile.

Slightly less malicious, but just as delicious, is the work of the Pioneer Quilters of Eugene, Oregon, who, in 1996, made the group quilt SUNBONNET SUE HAS A BAD DAY. The misfortunes that befall Sue range from annoyances (a skunk following her) to utter distress (stranded on a deserted island surrounded by shark-infested waters). Another quilt, SUNBONNET SUE COMES OF AGE, was assembled from first-place blocks from a 1995 quilt block contest sponsored by the Fairfield Processing Corporation. Clever little appliquéd scenes show Sue as an astronaut, veterinarian, and presidential candidate. Arlene Stamper's THE CENTURY QUILT, celebrating the millennium, updates Sue for each decade. In the 1970s, Sue wears a Saturday Night Fever suit and strikes a disco pose. In the block labeled "1980," she sweats as she rides her stationary bicycle. And for the final decade of the century and millennium, the familiar figure approaches a computer monitor that reads, "You've Got Mail, Sue."

By the end of the twentieth century, many quiltmakers had fallen in love, if not with Sunbonnet Sue, at least with appliqué. With heart, hand, and machine, contemporary stitchers were making quilts that were the rival of any masterpiece from the colonial, antebellum, or Depression eras.

THE SUN SETS ON SUNBONNET SUE
(62" × 78", 1979)
by the "Seamsters' Union (Local #500)."
Courtesy of Michigan State
University Museum.

Quilting Our Quilts: Traditions & Trailblazers

Hooray! My quilt top is finally done! The sense of accomplishment and relief that we quilters feel at reaching this milestone is momentous. However, it is invariably short lived, because we next have to face the fact that the hardest, most intimidating phase of quiltmaking is still ahead—the quilting.

The Pressure Is On

In the '70s, '80s, and '90s, almost every quilter felt pressured to finish her quilt beautifully. The expectation was that the quilting would be at least as long and labor-intensive as the work put into making the quilt top. Despite living in the modern age, quilters felt constrained by the same standards set by eighteenth- and nineteenth-century ladies of leisure: close crosshatching, graceful feathers, and perfect cables, each applied with infinitesimal hand-quilting stitches. Such quilting maintained its appeal and continues to generate admiration. Those with lofty aspirations and the means sought and found newly refined materials, tools, and expert teachers.

For the majority of quilters, however, several truths hit home. There wasn't enough time for heirloom-quality quilting, and it was wasted on utilitarian quilts with their daily wear and tear. Another concern was that the long,

BUTTERNUT SUMMER (81" x 81", 1998)
by Diane Gaudynski.
In the collection of the
Museum of the American Quilter's Society.

"The quilting is your signature, your handwriting; it's what puts you into your quilt."
                                    -Diane Gaudynski

"I think of quilting as the icing on a cake. When you make a cake, no matter how fresh and flavorful the ingredients or how carefully they are combined, the icing style tells you whether that cake will be served at a family picnic or a wedding reception. Like cake decoration, lots of hand quilting in intricate patterns says, 'This quilt is very special."

-Elsie Campbell,
from Winning Stitches

drawn-out process of hand quilting would lose the novice quiltmaker. Last but certainly not least, the quilt world came to realize that machine-quilted projects could be beautiful, too, even those that were quickly executed. All of these attitudes fueled the development of labor- and time-saving ways to finish a quilt. By the end of the twentieth century, "quilt as desired" referred to design, technique, and labor intensity.

Good, Better, Batts

For centuries, makers of battings have responded to and anticipated quilters' needs, and have consequently wielded a huge influence on the way quilts looked and felt. After all, a batt's composition and structure determine much of the final quilt's drape, texture, and weight.

In the early 1970s, quilters felt terribly proud of the texture and dimensionality of their handmade quilts in comparison with flat bedspreads and afghans. Many novices and quick quilters aimed for the puffiest results possible, simulating a European down comforter. Polyester fiber, developed in the early 1950s, has resilience, giving this type of batting a lot of depth and springiness. The names of the Dacron polyester battings that were new in the '60s and '70s said it all: "Hi-Loft" and "Fat Batt." Thrilled to be freed from the chore of quilting lines that were no more than one-quarter or perhaps one-half

TRIPLE TRIO OF STARS (90" x 90")
by Elsie Campbell.
Courtesy of C&T Publishing, Inc.
Photo by Sharon Risedorph.

inch apart (as required by the early 100 percent natural cotton battings), quiltmakers machine stitched rows as much as six inches apart, tied their quilts at intervals of up to ten inches, or joined rows of little stuffed pillows into quilts, called "puff" or "biscuit" quilts. (See Minnie Loeper's biscuit quilt on page 32.)

In her hilarious little gem of a book, *How Not to Make A Prize-Winning Quilt*, Ami Simms jokes about her humble beginnings in quilting. She remembers a time, early in her marriage, when she was only too happy to respond to her hubby's request for a warm bed quilt. She already had the completed patchwork quilt top, made predominantly of polyester blends, which she knew would "wear like cast iron," and the bed sheets for the backing, chosen because "they weren't doing anything." When it came time to quilt, she wrote, "I reasoned if one layer of Ultra Fluffy Quilt Batting wasn't warm enough, maybe two would be." With the quilt on the frame, she complained, "Working my needle through all that polyester, the percale sheets, and the double layer of batting was not fun. It was like trying to quilt through a sanitary napkin."

After a project or two, quilters' tastes evolved beyond the puffy looks, and there was a yearning to achieve the look of the old, thinner quilts. They got it with cotton batting. When teamed with new, unwashed quilt fabrics and washed for shrinkage, it gave a soft vintage look, though without careful planning, a quilter could be left with a quilt that hardly covered the bed. Still, expert quilters often chose polyester batts, selecting the newer varieties that were thin and easy to needle and that allowed them to do stippling, the densest quilting pattern of all.

"When I got into it, there were such high standards, and anything finely stipple-quilted was much admired."
-Charlotte Warr Andersen

Beastly Bearding

A big problem with the batts, especially the polyester ones, was their tendency toward "bearding," in which the batt's white fibers poked through dark fabrics. As one solution, Hobbs Bonded Fibers brought out dark-colored battings in the mid-1980s. At first, only the exteriors were dyed a slate gray color, but white fibers from inside migrated and broke through to the surface. Soon, an improved, all-dark batting became available. By 1996, a number of companies were offering batts that locked in the fibers with needle-punching, thermo-bonding, or synthetic finishes, all of which cut the bearding problem significantly, though not completely.

In 1996, Fairfield Processing Company brought out an 80 cotton/20 polyester blend of batting, offering quilters the best of all worlds. The cotton content allowed for a soft, drapable "hand," and it was easy to needle, while the polyester provided durability and the freedom to quilt less densely. Other companies picked up the cotton/poly batt and offered quilters many more choices in thickness, surface treatment, and fiber content. Mothproofing got the bugs out of the wool batts. Luxurious silk became available, though pricey and hard to find. Savvy quilt shop staff learned to help customers choose the best batting for the project, based on the quilt's end use, desired warmth and weight, and the type and amount of quilting that would go into it. Cotton was king before 1950, but with most quilters looking for the quick and easy throughout the '70s, '80s, and '90s, polyester and cotton/poly blends dominated the market.

Stencils went from cardboard to plastic.

Arrows on continuous-line quilting patterns or diagrams, like this one designed by Helen Squire, show the quilting path.

In the mid-1990s, fusible-backed battings came out. These iron-on "fleeces" and coated battings enticed and captivated consumers who felt pressed for time and were delighted to eliminate pinning or basting their quilt layers for their machine-quilting projects.

Paper or Plastic? Stencils and Patterns

In the early 1970s, quilters not only used the same designs as their colonial ancestors, but also the same types of stencils and patterns for applying the quilting design lines to the quilt top. The hand-cut cardboard or metal stencils that had been used for centuries were all that was available. But change was afoot. In 1971, Garrett Raterink began utilizing the same engraving machines that were used to perforate leather dress shoes to produce his plastic, machine-cut stencils. To this day, stencil companies cater to the quilter's every desire. Feather designs are the favorite, with cables a close second. Each year brings more variations, sizes, shapes, and styles of these classics for quilting.

Beginning in the 1980s, to satisfy quilters' desire for whimsy, especially for baby and children's quilts, design lines began to include teddy bears, bunnies, hearts, and flowers. In the 1990s, once free-motion quilting captured a following, quilters were eager to trace graceful, symmetrical motifs in machine stitches, without constant stops and restarts. Continuous-line quilting designs, first as patterns, then as stencils, became the new greatest hits.

Non-Marked Designs

Avoiding marking altogether, and with it the requisite time spent removing marks or apologizing for the marks that didn't come out, was a frequent goal. Several products arrived to accommodate quilters. Masking tape had long been called upon for applying straight-line guides, such as rows or grids (cross-hatching). Since quilting is often done ¼" from a seam, perfectionists used to purchase inch-wide rolls of tape from the hardware store and cut it down themselves. But in 1985, help arrived—a ¼" quilter's tape came on the market and was soon followed by a ⅛" width. On the tail of this success, Tiger Tape™ roared onto the market in the 1990s. Its crosswise printed marks offered quilters guidelines for evenly spaced quilting stitches. Resourceful quilters cut their own shapes from Con-Tac® paper. Also making their debut in the 1990s were self-adhesive motifs in hearts, flowers, and other simple shapes to quilt around or iron-on.

Design-It-Yourself

In the 1990s, most quilters continued to rely on commercial products and patterns for quilting designs, but confident quiltmakers altered and originated quilting designs to better suit their quilts. There were a number of methods to transfer original quilting designs or adapt other designs. Some were not neces-sarily developed for quilting, and they varied widely in sophistication. At one end of the spectrum there was freezer paper for transferring original designs onto quilt tops in preparation for quilting, and tissue-thin papers to quilt through and then tear away. At the other end were the high-tech helps—photocopiers and scanners to reduce, enlarge, and reproduce designs of one's own choosing. Quilting soft-ware and Internet resources allowed computer-techies to draft and adapt all sorts of linear designs for quilting.

Benchmarks for Markers

Marking quilts was a matter of deep impor-tance that presented many pitfalls and mine-fields. Most people chose to mark their quilts in sections as they proceeded, rather than before-hand, to avoid marks that could become a per-manent part of the quilt. The challenges of keeping a marking utensil sharp, getting a read-able line on dark fabric, avoiding having marks rub off, and above all, removing the marks after quilting had many a quilter searching, experi-menting, and pulling out her hair.

In 1970, the common #2 pencil was the common choice, but it smeared. The hera, a sharp-edged tool that had been around since the 1800s, scored a fine crease line, but the line could be permanent. Quilters also had dress-maker's chalk (which smeared and rubbed off), powdery pouncers (ditto), and a product like carbon paper called dressmaker's tracing paper (markings didn't come off). In 1978, markers arrived with a blue ink that could be washed out. They were joined by markers with thinner lines, different colored inks, and inks that disappear over time. Quilters had to use remarkable powers of memory, because heat applied inadvertently to such marks sets them permanently. Appearing in the early 1980s, the chalk-marking wheel was washable but unsuitable for elaborate designs. Silver pencils came out in the mid-1980s. Chalky enough to adhere, yet water-soluble, they often got the highest marks in surveys of quilters. However, they needed a firm surface, and like any marking tool, they didn't show up on every fabric. Each tool had its good and bad points and needed to be tested. To this day, the perfect marker remains the impossible dream.

Basting the Sandwich

The business of securing the layers of backing, batting, and quilt top involved another sometimes daunting chore, particularly for large quilts. Basting stitches or safety pins (inserted with the help of a spoon) were the choices of great grandmother and are still used. The mid- to late-1990s brought curved safety pins, specialized spoons and forks, pin closers for the safety pins, the basting or tacking gun to shoot thin plastic strands through the layers, adhesive sprays, and fusible batts.

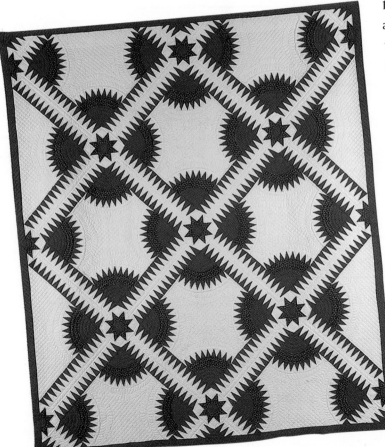

NEW YORK BEAUTY, detail,
by Martha B. Skelton
(77" x 90", 1986, see cover).
This quilt won first place in the Traditional
Pieced category at the 1987 AQS Show.
In the collection of the
Museum of the American Quilter's Society.

Help for the Hand Quilter

Throughout the three decades at the end of the twentieth century, hand quilters consistently strived for quality equaling or surpassing the handwork of their foremothers. They wanted to make stitches so fine that the texture was allowed to show but there was almost no sign of thread. That was the ultimate goal of the traditionalist.

Martha Skelton of Vicksburg, West Virginia, comes from a long line of Oklahoma quilters, and she made her first quilt in 1934 at the age of fifteen. She has always used cotton batting and works, on her own, on a large frame, so she can quilt by hand whenever she gets a few spare minutes. "I don't like my quilts puffy," she says, and to ensure a flatter look, she spaces her masking taped grid lines no more than 5/8" apart. She uses a #4 pencil to draw many of her own patterns, such as feathers, to achieve a greater density than commercial patterns would provide. Her hand-quilting stitches, in a thread to match the background, are tiny, even, and impeccable. "I want people to notice the pattern, not the thread," she explains. Although Martha has consistently been juried into the AQS Show since 1987 and has won many awards, she has a practical reason for pursuing the traditions: "I like hand quilting because it gives a soft appearance to your quilt in addition to the soft feel. I don't hang my quilts. Almost all of them are for beds, made to be touched, used, washed, and eventually worn out."

A good teacher, along with a lot of practice, was always of critical importance to the person who wanted to refine her skills. In the 1970s, people were lucky to have a family member, neighbor, or friend to teach them whatever cultural and regional methods were prevalent. Most quilters were working in isolation and developing their own individual solutions to problems. Help for thousands of them arrived in the mid-1970s and ran for twenty years—a regular feature written for *Lady's Circle Patchwork Quilts* titled, "Dear Helen, Can You Tell Me?" In this column, quilt-pattern designer and author Helen Squire answered quilting questions to "lead the reader on to the next level of quilting awareness." Beyond simply preaching even stitches, Helen helped with the decisions of "what to quilt, when to quilt it, and why."

Hoop Dreams

Since only a few, very dedicated hand quilters had the space at home for a quilt frame, most people sought another, more practical means of keeping their work taut. Anita Shackelford, a prizewinning hand quilter from Bucyrus, Ohio, looks back at what was around in the 1970s. "The hoops were certainly questionable—probably embroidery hoops at the time. There were square stretcher bars, too, the four strips with holes drilled through them, more like a needlepoint frame. Larger quilts went into a wooden hoop from Montgomery Ward."

Engineers applied their talents to designing a better hoop or frame. John Flynn of Montana is most famous for his award-winning quilts as well as his quilt frame business. As he tells it, "My wife, Brooke, was learning to quilt in 1979 and needed a quilt frame. In the process of designing the frame and testing it, I found out how relaxing hand quilting can be and proceeded to quilt Brooke's quilt for her and the next one, and the one after that."

Helen Squire's successful column helped quilters for 20 years.

John Flynn at his hand quilting in the early 1980s.
Photo by David Scott Smith

THOSE OUR HEARTS ARE FONDEST OF
(82" x 82", 1988-1991)
by Anita Shackelford.

Many quilters discovered methods for hand quilting without any stretching apparatus. Georgia Bonesteel, who made lap quilting a household term, preaches flexibility in attitude: "There are people who don't think you're quilting unless you use a hoop. I quilt with and without, two different ways. Whenever I visit a guild or teach a class, I always show both ways."

Other Handy Helps

Beginning in the mid-1980s, many other new tools and materials put tinier stitches within the reach of hand quilters. Manufacturers coated newer hand-quilting threads with silicone or glazes to allow them to glide through the layers and prevent tangling. A wider choice of needles was imported from Asia.

Metal thimbles remained an essential item, but they came with enticing additions, like needle grabbers and pushers, and some had a slot for a long fingernail to poke through.

Time to Relax

Throughout the decades, hand quilters have consistently strived for quality equaling or surpassing the handwork of our foremothers, but most devotees choose it and stay with it because they just love the process and are only too happy to rhapsodize about its therapeutic effects. For Anita Shackelford, it's a chance "to sit quietly at my work, even if I'm in front of a raucous football game." For Elsie Campbell, it has been a reward for a long day of teaching school and something to do while enjoying television with her family. "If I had quilted my quilts by machine," Elsie says, "I would have been isolated in my sewing room for hours on end." Charlotte Warr Andersen reminisces about putting a basted quilt in a frame and getting comfortable in an easy chair in the corner where she could "quilt for hours" with her "two little shadows," her dogs, at her feet.

Doctors sent patients to Didi McElroy and her mother, Roxanne, to learn "that perfect stitch" as physical therapy. "Hand quilting, done properly, can help people suffering from tendonitis, arthritis, or carpal tunnel syndrome," says Didi. " I love quilting, and even more, I love helping someone do what they've always wanted to do."

"The smallest needle was a #10, and when the #12 came along in the mid-'80s, I was absolutely thrilled. I could make much smaller stitches after that."

-Anita Shackelford

Magical Machine Quilting

Any newcomer endures some criticism. Some quilters will always turn their noses up at machine quilting. Others think it's a godsend. But one single event rocked the quilting world and changed the face of quilting forever. In 1989, CORONA II: SOLAR ECLIPSE, a machine-quilted masterwork, won the top prize at the American Quilter's Society show in Paducah, Kentucky, with a purchase award of $10,000. The artist, Caryl Bryer Fallert, remembers hearing the news. "It was stunning to me that this would win," she says. She was far from alone.

"You wouldn't believe the unkind things that some people said to Caryl's face after this win, but the artist's response was consistently and impeccably gracious. What a talent, and what a magnanimous grace."

-Darlene Zimmerman

CORONA II, SOLAR ECLIPSE
(76" x 94", 1989) by Caryl Bryer Fallert.
In the collection of the
Museum of the American Quilter's Society.

CORONA II, SOLAR ECLIPSE (detail).

But there were also positive responses to CORONA II. Caryl remembers, "For every one who fainted dead away, three people would come up and whisper in my ear, 'Thank goodness. Now, I can finish my quilt the way I want!'"

Even before Caryl won at Paducah, machine quilting was gaining acceptance. "In some respects I'm getting credit for blazing new territory, when in fact, I hadn't." Caryl explains, "In truth, mine was not the first machine-quilted piece to win big. Six months prior, in Houston, Lois Smith won a Best in Show with a machine-quilted quilt as well. But that one flew under the radar because it was a Christmas quilt of pieced blocks, basically traditional."

BLUE MEDALLION (68" x 84", 1984)
by Harriet Hargrave.
Detail to show stitching.
Photo by Brian Birlauf.

The win by CORONA II: SOLAR ECLIPSE is commonly regarded as the official turning point for most quilters. Since this event, there's been a quantum shift. Just four years afterward, prizes were awarded for both the best hand quilting and for the best machine quilting.

Winning Converts to Machine Quilting

Quilters anxious to achieve old-fashioned effects with their machine quilting were in luck when clear nylon thread became available in 1983. With newer machines and smaller machine needles, machine quilting became more refined in appearance, with greater evenness in the stitches and less noticeable needle holes. Two sewing machine features that had long been in existence were rediscovered for achieving an heirloom look. First was the even-feed, or walking foot, originally designed for handling home-decorating upholstery projects. Its ability to guide the quilt layers evenly produced a neater look for the back of the quilt. Second was the darning foot (used with lowered feed dogs), which had also been around for a century. With this foot, the home sewer could move her work in all directions to darn a hole. That same freedom of movement, or free-motion, allowed quilters to stitch backward, side to side, and in spirals and loop-de-loops over the surface of their layered quilts. Quilters began drawing traditional feathers, cables, and intricate curves of all kinds with the sewing machine. Continuous-line patterns for free-motion quilting offered traditional looks, but in faster time. A Mountain Mist® booklet captioned one quilt, "400 hours by hand vs. 40 hours by machine."

HOT FUN (56" x 63", 1995)
by Melody Johnson.
In the collection of the
Museum of the American Quilter's Society.

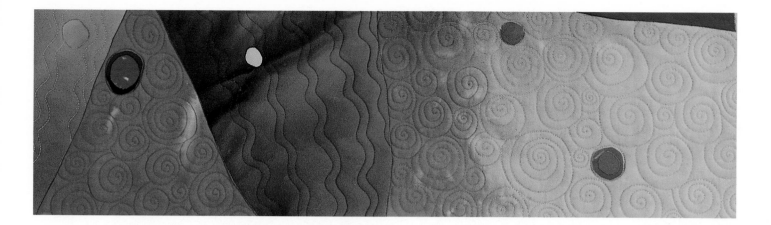

HOT FUN (detail).

The New Wave

Free-motion quilting went far beyond traditional looks. Those quilters seeking to emulate Caryl Bryer Fallert's style began using this technique with increasing freedom and eventually with wild abandon. Many quilters gave up marking, and quilted as if they were drawing freehand. Because quilters yearned to learn the secrets of high-flying effects, free-motion quilting was a popular class at quilt symposiums, festivals, and quilt shops.

In fact, machine quilting turned things around completely. Quilters felt liberated to try many exhilarating effects with their stitching, such as bobbin work, exemplified by Sharee Dawn Roberts; couching, which secured braids, cords, and other trims to the surface; and sashiko, simulating the Japanese art of hand-stitched designs. In addition, the look of trapunto rendered with new and faster techniques puffed up quilts and the quiltmaker's sense of pride.

As machine quilting began to come into its own, thread diversity exploded. At the end of the century, quilters had access to hundreds of colors including many variegated ones, and to various thicknesses, textures, and fibers. They could stitch in straight lines or use decorative machine stitches that embellished and quilted at the same time. Thread could be a prominent design element in a quilt as well as supplying intricate detail. Marci Brier, a marketing maven at A&E, distributor for Mettler® threads, sums up the shift, "It used to be that thread was meant to blend, to stay behind the scenes. Now it's often the star, a strong contrast to the fabric, providing a major role in the design, or a show-stopping form of embellishment."

"I have discovered that decent free-motion quilting only comes with practice and a song. I usually sing while I quilt because that helps me keep a consistent rhythm and motion with my hands. I also name many of my designs: there's the Me, Me, Me pattern, the Curly Fries, and the Bananas pattern. One of my favorite patterns is called Snails on Fire, but I prefer the more refined title of Escargot Flambé."

-Laura Wasilowski

Some quilting thread choices from 1970-2000.

FREDA'S STAR (83" × 83", 1999)
by Hari Walner.
Hari used her own trapunto techniques to
finish this quilt pieced by her grandmother,
Freda Remer Steiger (1884-1973), in the '40s.

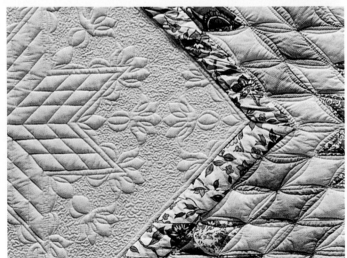

FREDA'S STAR (detail).

FLORET (40" x 40", 1999) by Laura Heine.
Photo by Larry Friar. In the collection of Linda Teufel.

Laura lavished a lot of
free-motion quilting on FLORET, (detail).

The Greatest Freedom of All

The biggest change? ... the freedom to forego the quilting phase altogether. No matter the era, tufting (tying the quilt at intervals) has always been a common, quick, and easy alternative to quilting, but if you wanted to quilt yet didn't have the time or skills, what then? The answer presented itself in the 1990s. A massive industrial sewing machine elbowed its way into the quilt world. It had been around in one form or another for more than 100 years and was used for quilting commercial bedspreads. Rollers hold the layers and sandwich them together as the quilt is quilted. Wheels and tracks allow the needle to travel anywhere. Monster or miracle, the longarm showed up at quilt shows, where quilters could gauge its potential and take a test drive.

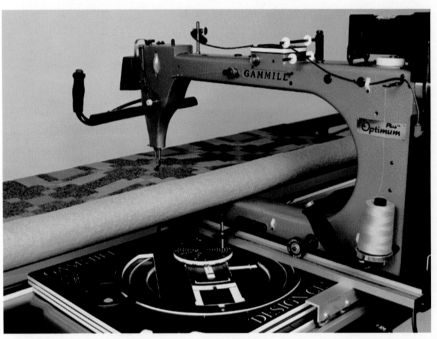

Longarms have revolutionized machine quilting.
Photo courtesy of Gammill Quilting Machine Company.

Longarms also created jobs. Many an individual or shop with the space and the down-payment installed a longarm, inviting customers to send them their quilt tops.

Linda Pumphrey, a quilt historian and sales manager at Stearns Technical Textiles Company reported, "Between 1970 and 1975, less than one percent of quilters handed their quilt tops over to professional quilters. In 1995, about 10 percent of quilters were sending quilt tops out to be commercially quilted on a longarm sewing machine. At the end of the twentieth century, that percentage is up to 40 percent."

Since the end of the century, quilters have no longer had to wield total control over their quilts. For some, this development has freed them to be more creative and productive. They can revel in the next phase of finishing or move right on to the next quilt. For others, technology has taken the heart out of the process, or they simply do not have the means to access the changes. Most likely the large, inclusive world of quilting will find ample room for all.

Art Quilts: Unleashing Creativity

Combining the words art and quilt begs the question, What is an art quilt? And furthermore, What is art? What are arts and crafts? What is folk art? What is fine art? And, what, in fact, is a quilt?

The craft versus art debate about quilts has surfaced time and time again for more than three decades now, with different arguments proposed and pontificated by every segment—if not every member—of the quilting community. A good deal of divisiveness has been inevitable, especially with regard to contest and exhibition eligibility, but since 1971, a number of special exhibitions—some within the art world, others at quilt symposiums or in books and quilting magazines—have generated a dialogue between the opposing sides. The ongoing deliberations have slowly wrenched popular opinion away from the strict adherence to tradition, broadened the definitions, and redefined the quilt. Since the end of the last century, the welcome mat has been out for innovation in personal expression. Quilts have won recognition as an art form.

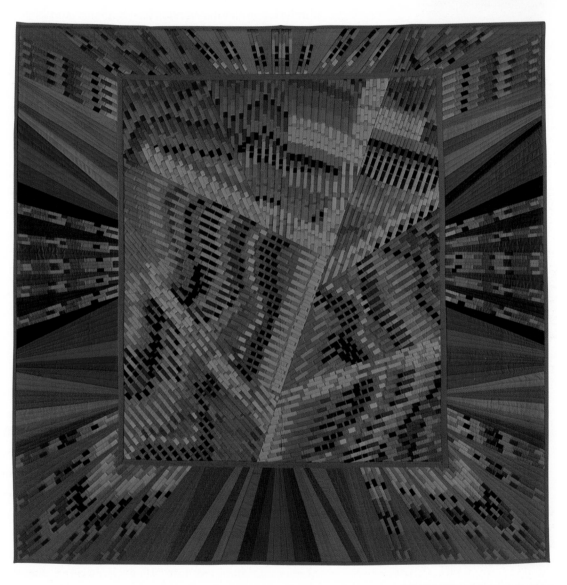

CELEBRATION (89" x 94", 1995) by Judith Larzelere.

Historic Connections

The original utilitarian object of quilts warming the bed is not always the goal of the contemporary quilter. Nonetheless, quiltmakers and the general public alike value the roots of quilting, and hearts are won over by good examples of classic antiques.

In 1968, Jonathan Holstein and Gail van der Hoof, both with a strong appreciation of modern art, started buying antique quilts on their weekend escapes from New York City. They chose bold, graphic designs—mostly pieced—that appealed to them, rarely paying more than $35 apiece for quilts purchased in Pennsylvania, New England, and New York State. Through connections in the art world, they were able to approach the Whitney Museum in New York City, which led quickly to an exhibition there. Like countless others, quilt historian Penny McMorris understood the importance of this momentous event, but summed it up with "udder" delight in the October '94 issue of *Quilter's Newsletter Magazine*: "In July 1971, the Whitney Museum took down a show of Andy Warhol's cow wallpaper and put up quilts from the Holstein/van der Hoof collection. The rest is history."

Each of the sixty-two quilts, dated between 1840 and 1930, had been made as a utilitarian bedcover. Many, in fact, featured less than wonderful workmanship, but hung on the walls of this modern art museum—the same walls that were usually given over to the outsized, minimalist paintings of the sixties. The parallels were clear. The title of the exhibit, Abstract Design in American Quilts (chosen after Up Against the Wall: Mother-Covers was wisely rejected), reinforced the connection.

In the years leading up to the bicentennial, Americans had begun to increase the value they placed on quilts, but the discerning museum-goer recognized that quilts could indeed operate on a similar plane as contemporary art. The hugely popular Whitney exhibit, portions of which traveled to various parts of the country and the world over the next few years, declared that quilts were no longer relegated solely to the category of handcrafts. Later, Amish quilts made between 1880 and 1940 made powerful visual statements on the walls

Abstract Design in American Quilts, an exhibition at the Whitney Museum of American Art, New York, 1971.
Photo by Jonathan Holstein, 1971.

of museums and corporate offices. Even more than the quilts in the Whitney exhibit, these patchwork masterpieces of rich, solid colors accented with black seemed on a par with the work of modern artists such as Mark Rothko, Kenneth Noland, and Brice Marden. Unfortunately, though most people looked at the antique quilts with new eyes, many still did not make the connection between contemporary quilts and art.

But, in fact, moving the quilt from bed to wall, from the horizontal to the vertical plane, was its ticket to fly as art. Seeing a quilt in its entirety, as opposed to getting a partial view of a quilt draped over a bed, gave the viewer the whole picture, a sense of the composition as a whole. In this way, any viewer could decide if the design succeeded in capturing attention and interest. And if a piece merited the designation of art, even utilitarian purpose could not rob it of this status.

From Amish Inspirations

Quilt artist Michael James had formal training as a painter and a printmaker, but after seeing classic Amish quilts, he turned his full attention to quiltmaking in 1973. Beginning by making meticulous, hand-pieced quilts, he followed traditions to educate himself. He soon turned to his own palette, lighter than that favored by his Amish precursors, and broke away from the most rigid formats to create new designs. In *The Quiltmaker's Handbook* (1978) and *The Second Quiltmaker's Handbook* (1983), he shared what he'd learned about construction and design. While he always injected an innovative, artful approach, he stayed true to strip-pieced blocks within a grid structure through most of the 1980s. In 1983 he wrote in an artist's statement, "My quilts are flexible supports for patterns painted with strips of fabric color." Gradually, he eliminated the underlying structure and any predictability that went with them. Since the end of the 1990s, Michael James has returned to elemental forms in new ways, with very sophisticated palettes. In 1993, he was inducted into the Quilters Hall of Fame. His work can be found in many significant art collections.

"The craft versus art debate on quilts? Controversy of any kind can ultimately be beneficial, since it often gives rise to questioning, to dialogue, to problem-solving, and to growth."

-Michael James

Someone to Crow About Quilts as Art

Like Michael James, Nancy Crow was inspired by classic Amish quilts. Another quiltmaker and teacher, she showed the quilt world how to forge a path to art. In the early 1970s, while seriously pursuing ceramics and weaving, Nancy taught herself machine-piecing. In 1976, quiltmaking became her medium of choice, and in 1979, she devoted herself to it full time. Log Cabin, Nine-Patch, Bow Tie, and Double Wedding Ring blocks served as springboards for original, innovative expression. In addition to pioneering rotary rulers, Nancy Crow has been generally credited with bringing the "design wall" to the attention of the quilt world. Just as the painter stands back to assess his work during various phases of design, any quilter making work that will eventually be hung up cannot compose effectively on a horizontal surface. On this large vertical surface, quilt elements can be temporarily stuck, pinned, moved around, or replaced, until a satisfactory design is reached.

Nancy Crow has produced an ever-evolving body of work. As she has worked through many series of pieced compositions, always leaving the finishing to an expert hand quilter, Nancy's work has become ever more abstract and exciting. Solo exhibits have appeared in several renowned art museums and some craft museums.

MEETING PLACE (45½" x 46", 1995)
by Michael James.
Photo by David Caras.

Nancy has sacrificed a great deal of time away from developing her own work in order to teach, but it is in this capacity that she has wielded an influence that goes far beyond her own art. Far more important than the tools, the techniques, and her body of work, Nancy Crow has introduced quilters to valuable principles of design and art. During a time when most quiltmakers timidly selected a limited palette of matching colors, Nancy nudged quilters toward an unrestrained use of color. Beginning in 1989, her annual Quilt Sur-

RED AND BLACK CROSSES
(64" x 78", 1971), by Nancy Crow.
Hand pieced and hand appliqued
by Nancy Crow and Rachel Crow.
Photo by J. Kevin Fitzsimons.

"I want to convey, more than anything, how the art of making a quilt must come from one's inner soul, how one's life experiences and perceptions must influence what one does, and to trust those feelings."

-Nancy Crow

face Design Symposium in Columbus, Ohio, has attracted serious quilters eager to become artists. While many students have attempted to reproduce the Nancy Crow look, her workshops are famous for challenging students to bring their unique individuality to the creative task.

INTERLACINGS III, (72" x 72", 1985)
by Nancy Crow.
Hand quilted by Rose Augenstein.
Photo by artist

LINEAR STUDY #9 (44" x 56½", 1995)
by Nancy Crow.
Hand quilted by Marla Hattabaugh
with pattern denoted by Nancy Crow.
Photo by J. Kevin Fitzsimons.

Art Quilts on the "Moo"-ve: The Birth of Quilt National

Despite the spread of innovative quiltmaking, most art quilts were still not accepted into mainstream quilt shows at the end of the 1970s. However, in 1979, opportunity knocked at the door of a barn—a dairy barn in Athens, Ohio, not far from Nancy Crow's home and studio. The space had once been a working dairy barn on the grounds of the local state mental hospital, providing milk and therapeutic work for the patients. The hospital had closed, and the dairy barn stood empty for ten years. It was nine days from the wrecking ball when philanthropists persuaded the governor to rescind the demolition order. In short order, the space was turned into a community arts center.

Nancy Crow, who was asked to teach there, recognized the barn's potential as an exhibit space for art quilts. For all the right reasons, and with the help of Cindy Rannels, Francoise Barnes, and other quilting pioneers, Quilt National was born. Prior to the deadline for that first quilt show in the summer of 1979, 196 artists submitted 390 slides of their work. Michael James, by that time well established as a quilt artist, was a judge, and fifty-six juried quilts were hung. The dairy barn had no screens on the windows, they didn't close properly, and there were flies everywhere. Conditions may have tried the patience of visitors, but the show created a buzz, touching off an explosive reaction to quilts as art.

Hilary Morrow Fletcher, who attended the first Quilt National and has been its director since 1983, thinks many of the quilts in that first show would be considered tame and traditional by today's standards. "That first Quilt National was so mild by comparison, almost transitional." That changed, however, in the very next show for this biennial forum, as did the number of quilters eager to participate. In 1991, the number of artists and submissions almost doubled, and it had tripled by 1999. The avant-garde quilts in the show have awakened an excitement in many people who weren't turned on by traditional quilts. Hilary comments, "It's so much fun to watch folks come through that door, especially the men. You can read the expression on their faces, 'I had no idea I was going to see this.'"

Visions of Art on the West Coast

Gradually, artistic quilts with original designs have become popular subjects for quilt exhibitions at other venues. On the West Coast, the guilds of the greater San Diego metropolitan area first organized Quilt San Diego in 1985, with the express goal of promoting quiltmaking as an art form. The regional focus expanded to an international one, and ten years later evolved into Quilt Visions. This show quickly established itself as a sophisticated biennial forum, alternating with Quilt National.

Frequent criticism took aim at quilts with sensational themes and others that didn't seem to qualify as quilts. The jurying philosophy, as stated in their catalogs, reads as a defense against such complaints: "We define a work of art as a work that is in some way extraordinary. It is expressive and invites us to see ourselves and the world anew, or inspires us in a new way.... It is certainly not our intention to shock the public ... it is important to represent the range of today's quiltmaking."

At a time when the vast majority of quiltmakers were focused on emulating classic quilts, Quilt National and Visions made a real impact on the greater quilt community. Other shows and contests began to include categories for, if not art quilts, at least innovative quilts and wall quilts. Art museums mounted shows of contemporary crafts or fiber art, with quilts routinely included. Arts publications, especially *Fiberarts* magazine, and several oversized, slick, coffee-table books trumpeted the masterpieces of artists working in the medium of quilting.

Straddling Both Worlds

Acceptance in both the worlds of craft and art is a high-wire act almost no one can master. Nancy Halpern, an early pioneer who prefers the label quilt-maker to artist, has come close. Her quiltmaking clearly shows that she honors the craft traditions of piecing and quilting, yet her designs are as personal, expressive, and evocative as any other art form. Nancy confesses, "I have a foot in two rafts, and they're pulling farther and farther apart."

A painter admittedly "hardwired into geometry," Nancy Halpern braved architecture school in the 1960s. She painfully remembers a time and place rampant with sexism. Because she had not been allowed to take any shop or woodworking classes in high school, she was at a serious disadvantage when drafting. Her professors and fellow students, all male of course, were of the opinion that she should "go home and make babies and leave architecture to us." But after making a quilt, she realized that she had found a way to satisfy her love of dimension and her need to construct models with geometric precision and artfulness. Nancy recalls, "For a few minutes I was an unhappy architecture student drop-out, but very soon thereafter, I was a happy quilter."

Nancy talks about her quilts as if they were her children, with minds and lives of their own. She confesses, "I want my quilts to have a strong identity." She values the interaction between creator and quilt, but also the one between quilt and viewer. "I love it when I have a dia-

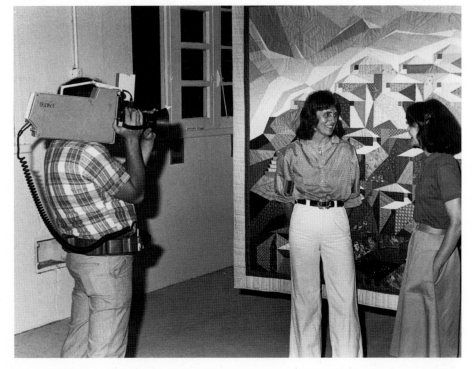

Nancy Halpern on Penny McMorris's TV show in the 1980s, with HILLTOWN behind her. Photo by Tim Westhoven.

logue with the quilts while I'm working on them, and then they have a dialogue with the viewer. My quilts are slow takes, but I want them to be the kinds that people have to study, the kinds that provoke a dialogue. I'm greedy with the viewer's time."

HOUSEWARMING (71" x 71", 1990)
by Nancy Halpern.
Photo by David Caras.

HOPPER (76" × 57", 1992)
by Nancy Halpern.
Photo by David Caras.

ARCHIPELAGO, (96" × 72", 1983)
by Nancy Halpern,
Designated one of the
Twentieth Century's 100 Best American Quilts.
Photo by David Caras.

Solid Bodies of Pieced Work

Along with Nancy Crow, Michael James, and Nancy Halpern, many artists who appeared on the scene in the 1980s dazzled viewers with their pieced abstractions. Judith Larzelere produced narrow strip-sets in deliberate color palettes, merging angled sections in huge formats (see page 111). Pamela Studstill incorporated minute, meticulous paint strokes into her complex strip-pieced latticework. Rhoda R. Cohen, Sylvia Einstein, and Ellen Oppenheimer each developed a unique and personal style of angular constructions overlaid with emotional associations. Judi Warren Blaydon softened her strong compositions with simple images. Miriam Nathan-Roberts played with gradations of fabrics for shimmering effects of light and illusive dimension.

CHARIVARI (59" x 59", 1986) and detail
by Sylvia H. Einstein.
Photo by David Caras.

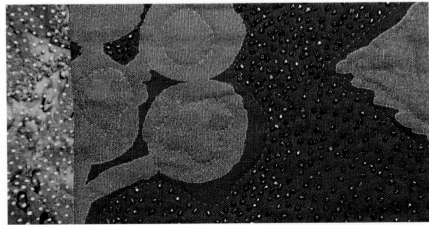

DRESS: FOR TEA AT THE RITZ
(34" x 54¼", 1997) and detail
by Judi Warren Blaydon.
Photo by Karen Bowers/Shoot for the Moon.

LATTICE INTERWEAVE (84" X 84", 1983)
by Miriam Nathan-Roberts.

Evolutions

Several quilt artists have journeyed a long way as their work diversified and developed, and those of us who have followed their careers had an inspiring ride. Yvonne Porcella brought a California exuberance to her pieced and appliquéd art quilts, which grew out of her wearable art (see pages 133–134). Starting in the late 1960s, she accented brilliant colors with hard-edged black-and-white graphics that smacked of op art, and then in the 1990s, she moved to works of painted silk that whisper of delicacy and impressionism. Francoise Barnes explored bold, grid-based constructions, then added graphic curves as she moved into a giant bug series. Erika Carter began with strip-pieced mosaics, then added appliqué, paint, and stamping to evoke a romantic landscape of the mind. Ruth McDowell pieced commercially available prints, plaids, and hand-dyes, creating pictorials that range from folktale charmers to works of rich, organic expressiveness.

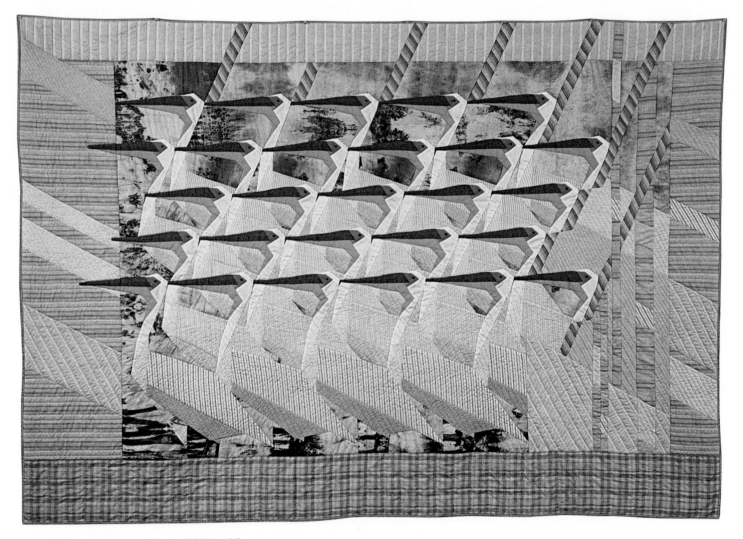

WHITE PELICANS AT LAKE EDWARD
(70" x 96", 1984) by Ruth B. McDowell.
Photo by David Caras.
Collection of Anna Pascuito.

Quilt historian Judy Roche strongly suggests, "If you want to study the quilting history of the '70s, '80s, and '90s, study the career of Chris Wolf Edmonds." From the beginning of the quilt revival in the early 1970s to the late 1990s, Chris Wolf Edmonds experimented with a gamut of techniques, moving from breathtaking pictorials in appliqué (see pages 74–75) to pieced marvels that owed their sophisticated, abstract artistry to paint and printing techniques as much as to piecing and quilting.

Many other artists have married their work with painting, without divorcing themselves from quilting. Linda MacDonald pieced and appliquéd abstracts of solid-colored fabrics with dimensional illusion in the art quilts she produced in the early 1980s. In 1987, she first incorporated thin lines of paint to move the viewer's eye along the surface of her quilts, and soon after that, she began devoting whole-cloth surfaces to painting techniques.

Visionaries

The quilt world lays claim to several people who may be academically trained, yet work in a style that is unrestrained and intuitive. Using a bounty of unusual embellishments, they are creating the most innovative, "out there" art. From the late 1980s through today, Terrie Hancock-Mangat, Jane Burch Cochran, and Susan Shie have had the inside edge among these outside the box artists.

Jane Burch Cochran makes up compositions as she goes along, heaping images and text over a classic quilt format. COMING HOME: KENTUCKY WOMEN QUILT is a brilliantly colored Log Cabin, featuring dozens of names, hundreds of buttons, gloves, painting and stamping, and a riot of colors.

Susan Shie, who goes by the nickname Lucky, has a Bohemian and romantic outlook on life and uses the quilting process as a running journal of her feelings and experiences. Her husband, James Acord, used to collaborate on many of her pieces, contributing his hand-tooled leather and other hardware embellishments. Such items join a huge array of collectibles and found objects, which add a sumptuous tactile quality. Since Lucky is legally blind, the sense of touch

GRACE (45" x 69", 1993)
by Erika Carter.

COMING HOME: KENTUCKY WOMEN QUILT
(78" × 81", 1994)
by Jane Burch Cochran,
Photo by Pam Monfort.

is an essential element of her work. Domestic joys are celebrated in RAIN-BOW GARDEN–A GREEN QUILT, in which a host of spoons, painted with smiling faces, symbolize abundance. Lucky contrasts her quiltmaking with her gardening: "In the garden, there must be some order, but in making art, one can jump around more. Though the final look of the quilt was unknown at the start, it grew together like a garden of weeds! We work better that way! The six months it took to fully harvest our garden was also the time it took to create this art quilt."

RAINBOW GARDEN–A GREEN QUILT
(94" × 78", 1996")
by Susan Shie and James Acord.
Photo by B&B Studios, Athens, Ohio.

I'LL FLY AWAY (82" × 92", 1991)
by Michael A. Cummings.
Photo by Sarah Wells, NYC.
Collection of the
Museum of Arts and Design (NYC).

CINDERELLA (77" × 87", 1995)
by Kyra E. Hicks.
Photo by David Smalls.

Artists of Color

One of the first quilt artists to be accepted into the fine art world was Faith Ringgold. Even though she has also created paintings on canvas throughout the last two and a half decades, Faith is best known for her quilts, which occupy places in the most prestigious museums and private collections. She is a storyteller, and the fabric surfaces of her quilts are covered with painted images and text, expressing a wide range of human emotion as seen through the lens of the African American experience. TAR BEACH centers on a family relaxing on a New York City rooftop, escaping the heat of a summer night. The artist's alter ego flies overhead, evoking the dreams and folktales of the slavery era. Another masterwork, SHADES OF ALICE, describes the tale of an African-American Alice who follows a white rabbit from Harlem down a rabbit hole, only to reappear in a strange inner city with no sky.

Since the late 1970s, white scholars discovered and conferred authenticity on the work of a group of elderly southern black women. Anna Williams, for example, won a following for her scrappy masterpieces, but only a few African American quilt artists were able to break free of the constrained expectations and receive recognition for other exciting explorations of heritage and experience. Wini Akissi McQueen and Elizabeth Scott did it in the 1980s. Peggie Hartwell and Michael Cummings followed in the mid-1990s. However, most contemporary quilters, particularly younger women, often felt discounted and disenfranchised by scholars and by the greater public. Quiltmaker Carolyn Mazloomi has been a liberating influence in the African American art community and a heroine of empowerment. The force behind the Women of Color Quilters Network, author of *Spirits of the Cloth*, and creator of the traveling exhibition with the same name, Carolyn has inspired black quilters to put their work in the public eye. This attention has created an audience for a younger generation, such as Kyra Hicks, Edjohnette Miller, Carole Lyles Shaw (see pages 42–43), and Frances Hare, and also quelled some misconceptions of what black quilts should and shouldn't be.

The Surface Reigns Supreme

Surface design techniques, like brushing, airbrushing, silk screening, stenciling, and painting with dyes, arrived on the scene in the 1980s to the acclaim of the art world, and they

"Let it be known that it is the quiltmakers, and not anyone else, who determine what the quilt art of their time and culture will be. Let it also be known that African American quiltmaking is an American art and is as rich and diverse as we are as a people."

-Faith Ringgold

in the preface to Spirits of the Cloth:
Contemporary African American Quilts,
by Carolyn Mazloomi (Clarkson Potter, 1998).

SHADES OF ALICE, (58" × 56", 1989/93)
by Faith Ringgold. Acrylic on canvas.
(Created in 1989, modified in 1993.)
Collection of the American Craft Museum, NYC.

have dominated the art quilt scene ever since. Jan Myers-Newbury and Debra Millard Lunn, who studied textiles in college together, are the leaders in techno-virtuosity. Early in their separate careers, Jan combined flat color in pieced mosaic designs, while Debra's concentration was on creating specialty fabrics. In the 1990s, both began experimenting with pigments and bleach, potato-pulp, PVC pipe, and tie-dye, creating art quilts with streaked and crackled surfaces that seem to owe their visual textures to alchemy rather than art or science.

A few others pioneered surface design in the '80s: Wenda Von Weise first garnered attention for photo transfer, followed by Elizabeth A. Busch, M. Joan Lintault, and Therese May, each of whom expanded the repertoire of photographic techniques combined with paint, dye, piecing, appliqué, and quilting. Karen Felicity Berkenfeld printed fabrics at home with linoleum blocks and stamps, and she pieced them together with bold African textiles and bright commercial prints. Robin Schwalb and Gerry Chase brought an array of images and text to their designs, made by using silk screen and photo-transfer techniques. Patricia Malarcher also used photo transfer for her distinctive patchworks, which frequently include Mylar and metal. Tafi Brown made blue her signature color. By exposing specially painted surfaces to ultra-violet light, she created blueprints for the focal areas of her pieced designs.

LET X=X (72" x 39", 1986) by Robin Schwalb. Photo by eeva-inkeri.

Painting New Directions for Art Quilts

Many quilt artists came from a painting background. Katie Pasquini Masopust was a painter before she was a quilter. In the early 1980s, she explored rounded forms and esoteric symbolism in her mandala quilts, gradually playing more and more with dimensional illusions. In the early '90s, Katie introduced the quilt world to isometric perspective, an unreal, other worldly dimension in which objects appear to float. Moving on to landscapes, she fractured images from vacation snapshots to add dream-like transparency. In each phase, she authored a how-to book and taught workshops to share her latest ideas with quilters.

During college, Caryl Bryer Fallert worked mostly in abstracts, using acrylics, but something was always lacking. "I was never able to actually get the colors that I wanted in my paintings. Plus, you're somewhat removed from the actual painting. Unless you're finger-painting, you're not handling the medium directly, as you are in quiltmaking."

Caryl went through several different series, always carving out her own special niche. Whether medallions, picture quilts, or flower quilts, her work is always beautiful to look at as well as technically impressive. Her awards are too numerous to mention, but among them are an unprecedented three Best of Show awards at the annual AQS Quilt Show in Paducah—CORONA II: SOLAR ECLIPSE (page 104), 1989; MIGRATION #2, 1995; and BIRDS OF A DIFFERENT COLOR, 2000.

"Whether it's a tole-painted chest of drawers, a painted canvas, or a patchwork quilt, it's still art. Just because the traditional mode is utilitarian doesn't preclude its use as a medium for art."

-Caryl Bryer Fallert

Emerging in the Nineties

The 1990s exploded with a lot of up-and-comers who developed their art as they worked on a series of quilts. Some trends that emerged from this era include pieced constructions in which the fabrics were selectively cut to create special effects; surfaces embellished with paint and other pigments; a profusion of fused appliqué; layering with unusual textures and stitching; and photo transfers and found objects.

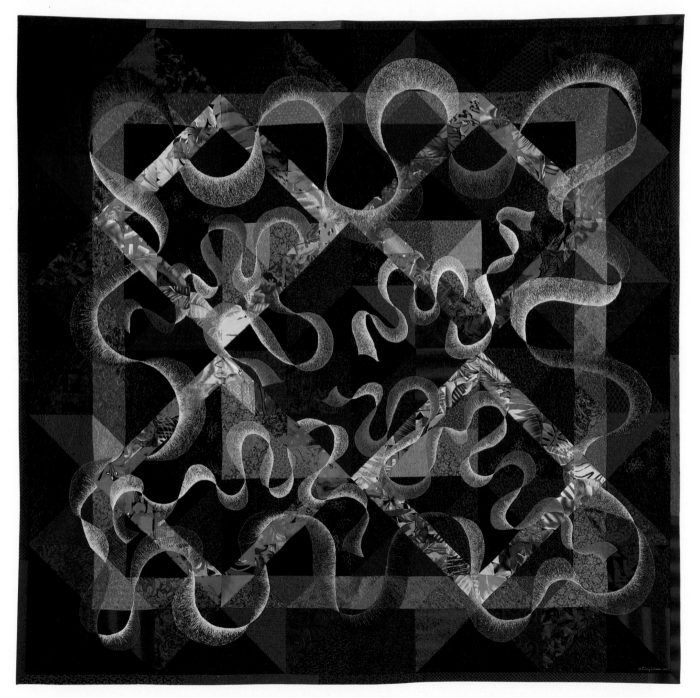

ESCAPADE (81" × 81", 1993)
by Libby Lehman.
From the collection of the
Museum of the American Quilter's Society.

SAHEL (60" x 80", 1997) by Hollis Chatelain.
Photo by Seth Tice-Lewis.

"Art quilters are moving into an era of deconstruction. Fusibles, along with air- or water-soluble products decrease the need for basting, battings, and bindings. Traditional piecing no longer dominates the construction process. The turned edges of direct and reverse appliqué are gradually disappearing in favor of raw edges. Artists are painting, dyeing, and printing their own fabric, using pieces to generate complex designs previously unimagined. Inner vision is the vehicle that transports artists into zones of experimentation."

-Barbara W. Watler

GULL POND (50" x 36", 1996)
by Carol Anne Grotrian.
Photo by David Caras.

Art to Wear

Quilts that conform to the shape of the human body have also gained acceptance as art. The kimono's voluminous, boxy shape provides a large area for design. When not being worn, it can be hung on a rod like a long, reversible triptych. In fact, its overall shape with the negative space beneath the elongated sleeves suggests a quilt with cutouts for the posters at the foot of the bed. The kimono, at once ancient and modern, is a popular subject for wearable art, timeless enough to ride through every decade. In the 1970s, Yvonne Porcella endowed the kimono shape with a palette of intense colors set off by black and white, and sometimes accented with metallic lamé. Yvonne soon transferred the same palette and energy to her art meant exclusively for the wall.

"My original inspiration was a large kimono seen in a museum exhibit. The sign said Bedding in Kimono Form! For me the kimono is like a moving sculpture, the front and back seen at different times."

-Yvonne Porcella

HOW TO ENJOY HOUSEWORK (30" x 39", 1999)
by Cynthia Myerberg.
Photo by M. Gregory Ellis,
West Virginia University Photographic Services.

ROBE FOR A DRAGONRIDER,
(48" x 60", 1982) by Yvonne Porcella.
Photo by Elaine F. Keenan.

An artist who routinely wears her theatrical creations, Virginia Avery is known for sweeping through the aisles at quilt shows, attracting hugs and admiration. She is frequently outfitted in one of her wrap coats, swing coats, or kimonos, accessorized to the nines with matching hat and bag. In the introduction to her 1982 book *Quilts To Wear*, Virginia presented a compelling argument for creating garments. She reasoned that, to get recognition and praise for your quilt, you have to invite your friends over, clean your house, and serve the appropriate refreshments. "This may be more than you bargained for, but it is also something you need not be concerned about if you direct your energies toward quilted clothes. You simply wear your handiwork and go wherever the action is. What you wear proclaims your talent more boldly than a billboard."

When Karey Bresenhan requested a special event to add excitement to the first Quilt Market in 1979, Concord Fabrics and Fairfield Processing Corporation responded with a fashion show. That first year, the organizers designed and hired garments to be made, which were all reflective of classic quilts. To widen the appeal of the show beyond shop owners, subsequent shows of The Fairfield Fashion Show, as it came to be known, included invitational work from celebrities and emerging talents in the wearable art world. Virginia Avery was the first artist recruited to submit wearable art. Until the end of its tenure, Fairfield required some use of its batting, which practically guaranteed that garments would feature quilting.

DON'T SHOOT THE PIANO PLAYER,
SHE'S DOING THE BEST SHE CAN
by Virginia Avery.

"From its simple beginning, The Fairfield Fashion Show has evolved into a much anticipated, annual event. It appeals to everyone who wields a needle and to some who don't know how to replace a missing button. Energy and art flourish and converge on the runway."

-Virginia Avery

Accessible Art

While "art to wear" is perhaps the most popular form of the genre, all quilt art is, by the nature of its traditions, accessible as art. The tactile qualities of the medium appeal to the soft spot in the heart and endear the art quilt to devotees of soft sculpture. The fact that quilts have historically warmed the bed—the center of birth, love, family, and death—endows the contemporary art quilt with layers of meaning, and because quilting comes from the domain of women's work, the value of women is often an underlying statement in art quilts.

"Now both quiltmakers and non-quilt-makers are beginning to understand that there is absolutely no difference between what today's quiltmakers are doing and what our great grandmothers did decades ago. They are using available materials and techniques to express their individual creativity and make tangible, long-lasting statements about themselves and their world."

-Hilary Fletcher
from the Best Contemporary Quilts:
Quilt National, 2001

Photos are courtesy of The Fairfield Fashion Show, produced by Fairfield Processing Corporation.

Saw Grass Fire by Ann Boyce.
From "Starburst," the 1985 Fairfield Fashion Show.

Dance Electric by Susan Deal.
From "Superstar," the 1988 Fairfield Fashion Show.

Bibliography

Periodicals:

American Quilter, American Quilter's Society, P.O. Box 3290, Paducah, KY 42002-3290. Phone: 270-898-7903; FAX: 270-898-1173; Web site: www.aqsquilt.com.

Quilter's Newsletter Magazine, Primedia Special Interest Publications, 741 Corporate Circle, Suite A, Golden, CO 80401. Phone: 303-278-1010; Web site: www.qnm.com.

Books and Catalogues:

Austin, Mary Leman, ed. *The Twentieth Century's Best American Quilts*. Golden, CO: Primedia Special Interest Publications, 1999.

Avery, Virginia. *Quilts to Wear*. New York: Charles Scribner's Sons, 1982.

—. *The Big Book of Appliqué*. New York: Charles Scribner's Sons, 1978.

—. *Wonderful Wearables*. Paducah, KY: American Quilter's Society, 1991.

Barnes, Christine. Color, *The Quilter's Guide*. Bothell, WA: That Patchwork Place, 1997.

The Best in Contemporary Quilts: Quilt National, 1999. Asheville, NC: Lark Books, 1999.

The Best Contemporary Quilts: Quilt National, 2001. Asheville, NC: Lark Books, 2001.

Beyer, Jenny. *The Art and Technique of Creating Medallion Quilts*. EPM Publications, 1987.

Bonesteel, Georgia. *Lap Quilting with Georgia Bonesteel*. Birmingham: Oxmoor House Inc., 1982.

Bradkin, Cheryl Greider. *Basic Seminole Patchwork*. Mountain View: Leone Publications, 1990.

Contemporary Quilts: Quilt National, 1997. Ashville, NC: Lark Books, 1997.

Campbell, Elsie. *Winning Stitches: Hand Quilting Secrets, 50 Fabulous Designs, 4 Quilts to Make*. Lafayette, CA: C&T Publishing, 2004.

Crow, Nancy. *Work in Transition*. Paducah, KY: American Quilter's Society, 1992.

Dale, Judy B. *Curves in Motion: Quilt Design Techniques*. Lafayette: C&T Publishing, 1998.

Dietrich, Mimi. *Basic Quiltmaking Techniques for Hand Appliqué*. Bothell, WA: That Patchwork Place, 1998.

Doak, Carol. *Easy Machine Paper Piecing*. Woodinville, WA: Martingale & Co., Inc. 1994.

Duke, Dennis, and Deborah Harding, eds. *America's Glorious Quilts*. New York: Hugh Lauter Levin Associates, Inc., 1987.

Faoro, Victoria A., ed. *MAQS Quilts: The Founders Collection*. Paducah, KY: American Quilter's Society, 2001.

Hargrave, Harriet. *From Fiber to Fabric: The Essential Guild to Quiltmaking Fabrics*. Lafayette, CA: C&T Publishing, Inc., 1997.

—. *Mastering Machine Applique*, Lafayette, CA: C&T Publishing, Inc., 2002.

The Hawaiian Quilt. Catalog to an exhibition curated by Reiko Mochinaga Brandon for the Honolulu Academy of Arts, Kokusai Art. Tokyo, 1996.

Heine, Laura. *Color Fusion: Fiberworks by Laura Heine*. Columbus, OH: Dragon Threads, 2001.

Holstein, Jonathan. Abstract Design in American Quilts: Biography of An Exhibition. Louisville, KY: The Kentucky Quilt Project, 1991.

Hopkins, Mary Ellen. *The It's Okay If You Sit on My Quilt Book*. Atlanta, GA: Yours Truly, 1982.

Horton, Roberta. *The Fabric Makes the Quilt*. Lafayette, CA: C&T Publishing, Inc., 1995.

James, Michael. *The Quiltmaker's Handbook: A Guide to Design and Construction*. Mountain View: Leone Publications, 1978.

James, Michael. *The Second Quiltmaker's Handbook: Creative Approaches to Contemporary Quilt Design*. Mountain View: Leone Publications, 1978

Johannah, Barbara. Quick Quilting. New York: Drake Publishing, 1976.

—. *The Quick Quiltmaking Handbook*. Menlo Park, CA: Pride of the Forest Press, 1979.

Kimball, Jeana. Reflections of Baltimore. Woodinville, WA: Martingale & Co., Inc. 1989.

Laury, Jean Ray. *Appliqué Stichery*. New York: Van Nostrand Reinhold, 1966.

—. *Imagery on Fabric: A Complete Surface Design Handbook*. Lafayette, CA: C&T Publishing, Inc., 1997.

—. *Quilts & Coverlets, a Contemporary Approach*. New York: Van Nostrand Reinhold Company, 1970.

Marshall, Suzanne. *Take-Away Appliqué*. Paducah, KY: American Quilter's Society, 1998.

Mazloomi, Carolyn. *Spirits of the Cloth: Contemporary African American Quilts*. New York, NY: Clarkson Potter, 1998.

McMorris, Penny, and Michael Kile. *The Art Quilt*. New York, NY: McGraw-Hill/Contemporary Books, 1996.

Mountain Mist Blue Book of Quilts, Celebrating 150 Years of Perfect Quilting. The Stearns Technical Textiles Company, publisher.

Nickels, Sue. *Machine Appliqué: A Sampler of Techniques*. Paducah, KY: American Quilter's Society, 2001.

Papadakis, Brenda Manges. *Dear Jane: the Two Hundred Twenty-five Patterns from the 1863 Jane A. Stickle Quilt*. West Warren, MA: EZ Quilting, Wrights, 1996.

Quilt National (compiler). *The Quilt: New Directions for an American Tradition*. Exton, PA: Schiffer Publishing Ltd., 1984.

Quilt National. *Fiber Expressions: The Contemporary Quilt*. West Chester, PA: Schiffer Publishing Ltd., 1987.

Reinstatler, Laura, ed. *Fine Art Quilts: Work by Artists of the Contemporary Quilt Art*. Bothell, WA: That Patchwork Place, Inc., 1997.

Reynolds, Bethany S. *Magic Stack-n-Whack® Quilts*. Paducah: American Quilter's Society, 1998.

Rogers, Janet, ed. *Visions: Quilt Art*. Visions catalogue. Lafayette, CA: C&T Publishing Co., 1996.

Shaw, Robert. *Quilts: A Living Tradition*. New York: Hugh Lauter Levin Associates, 1995.

Siekiewicz, Elly. *Spoken Without a Word*. Elly Sienkiewicz publisher, 1983.

Simms, Ami. *How Not to Make A Prize-Winning Quilt*. Lafayette, CA: C&T Publishing Co., 1994.

Townswick, Jane, ed. *Creative Guide to Color & Fabric*. Rodale's Successful Quilting Library Series. Emmaus, PA: Rodale Press, 2000.

Twentieth Century's Best American Quilts. *Quilter's Newsletter Magazine* and International Quilt Festival, 1999.

Webster, Marie. *Quilts: Their Story and How to Make Them*. Farmington Hills, MI: Gale Group, 1972.

Wahlman, Maude Southwell. *Signs and Symbols: African Images in African American Quilts*. New York: Penguin Studio, in association with the Museum of American Folk Art, 1993.

About the Author

Since her early childhood in Baltimore, Maryland, Eleanor Levie has enjoyed many diverse forms of sewing, weaving, and stitchery. In the 1970s, after five years as a secondary English teacher in urban public schools, she combined her hobbies and her instructional career to become a needlework and craft editor. Her first job at the *Woman's Day* special interest magazines was followed by senior positions at *McCall's Needlework & Crafts*, *Woman's World*, and *Country Accents*. Early in the 1980s, Eleanor made her first quilt for the bed of the first home she and her husband shared. She quickly confesses it was the first, and possibly the last, full-sized quilt she will ever make, though she works on smaller quilt projects whenever she gets the chance.

Eleanor authored *Great Little Quilts*, *Creations in Miniature*, co-authored *Country Living's Country Quilts*, and produced eight volumes of the *Rodale's Successful Quilting Library* series. In addition, she has edited dozens of quilt books and needlework magazines, writing copy and directions, and styling the photography. Since 2002, she has shared her passion for quilts, both yesteryear's classics and today's innovative masterpieces, as a lecturer for guilds and study groups. Her patchwork career also includes leading diverse craft and embellishing workshops—some for quilters, others for kids. She lives with her husband and their son in Doylestown, Pennsylvania.

TIMELINE, (40½" × 30", 2003), by the author, was created especially for this book.

Other AQS Books

This is only a small selection of the books available from the American Quilter's Society. AQS books are known worldwide for timely topics, clear writing, beautiful color photos, and accurate illustrations and patterns. The following books are available from your local bookseller, quilt shop, or public library.

#6415   us$29.95

#6036   us$24.95

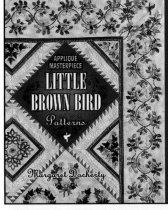

#5338   us$21.95

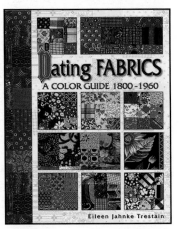

#4827   us$24.95

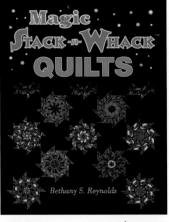

#4995   us$19.95

#6204   us$19.95

#6009   us$19.95

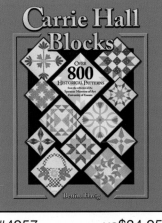

#4957   us$34.95

#5883   us$24.95

LOOK for these books nationally. **CALL** **1-800-626-5420**

or **VISIT** our Web site at **www.AQSquilt.com**